Praise for *Living with Twelve Men*

Funny. Poignant. Heartwarming. *Living with Twelve Men*, Betty
Auchard's third memoir, takes us on her journey, which begins in the late
1940s. She marries and looks for the woman she'll become, who is the
marvelously funny and artistic person we met as a new widow in *Dancing
in My Nightgown*. In her memoirs, Auchard's prose is irresistible,
drawing you in and not letting go until the tale is told.

Matilda Butler, author of *Rosie's Daughters:
The "First Woman To" Generation Tells Its Story*

Living with Twelve Men is a fascinating set of stories that picks up after
Betty Auchard's previous memoir, *The Home for the Friendless*. Now
she tells of her first teenage dates, the joy of finding her mate for life,
and the complexities of marrying a minister's son. The couple moves to
a strict church college campus, where her new roles as a faculty wife
and housemother to twelve young men require an attitude adjustment.
As a preacher's kid, I shared her feelings about restrictions in a social
environment where dancing and alcohol were forbidden. Betty doesn't
shy away from sharing in a humorous way the most intimate and
sometimes embarrassing situations that characterized her life with her
husband, Denny. Her most compelling stories are about becoming a
mother. In hilarious detail, we read how she and her husband conceived
their first child. Following her passage from a nineteen-year-old bride to
a faculty wife and mother kept me thoroughly engrossed.

Dr. Robert L. Spaulding, *retired professor, San Jose State University*

Auchard's book is a quaint look at small-town living in midcentury
America. Though it depicts a bygone era, it has timeless themes—
coming of age, young love, new parenthood—that make it highly relevant
to today's audience. It is a delightful read.

Chrystal Houston, Director of Alumni
and Communication, York College, NE

Betty's stories show her as a determined, sensitive, caring child/woman
who adapted to anything the world sent her.

Carol Medsker, York College Alumna

These stories are like an episode out of a good novel. You would not have to know the characters to appreciate the experiences and, most likely, you'll be reminded of your own past. People in the Midwest, in the days leading to our own time, were survivors. We're used to hearing, "Forget the past," but maybe it's not so bad to remember the past if in it one finds pleasant memories and laughter. Betty does that with both dignity and grace. I would recommend that you read the story to see for yourself.

Dr. J. Benton White, *retired professor, San Jose State University*

Reading a Betty Auchard memoir is like being there with her. First, there was *Dancing in My Nightgown: the Rhythms of Widowhood*, a series of short stories chronicling her life after her husband of forty-nine years passed away. Then there was *The Home for the Friendless*, a memoir of her childhood, and what a childhood it was. Now there is *Living with Twelve Men*. We move forward with Betty into the early years of her married life. Betty combines poignant moments with lighthearted and humorous anecdotes. Take it from an avid reader and reviewer, I will always be the first in line to buy a Betty Auchard book. You might want to think about doing the same.

Lloyd Russell, www.booksageblogspot.com

Betty was born to write, even though she may not have figured that out until later in life. A captivating storyteller, she lures you in from the first sentence, and no matter how old you are, or in what era you grew up, you can identify with the thoughts and events she recounts with humor, poignancy, and great insight.

Nina L. Diamond, journalist, essayist, author, and former Independent Publisher Book Awards (IPPY Awards) judge, 2004-2011.

Betty, your stories are begging to be told—not only for their humor but because they contain the key themes in your book: an insistence on living life brightly and touching each other through the heart.

Bruce McAllister, consultant, writing coach, mentor, agent finder, author, and owner of McAllisterCoaching.com

Living with
Twelve Men

Also by Betty Auchard:

Dancing in My Nightgown: The Rhythms of Widowhood
(Available in Spanish as: *Bailando in mi camisón: Al compás de la vindez*)

The Home for the Friendless: Finding Hope, Love and Family

Living with Twelve Men

... a mother in training

Betty Auchard

Living with Twelve Men

ISBN: 978-1-61170-228-6

Edited by Sandi Corbitt-Sears

Book design and production by Sue Campbell

Illustrations by Betty Auchard

First Printing

Published by:

 Robertson Publishing™
Fremont, California USA
www.RobertsonPublishing.com

Printed in the USA and UK on acid-free paper.
To purchase additional copies go to:

    amazon.com

    barnesandnoble.com

Dedicated to:
Carl and Glenna Bott
Carolyn Hayes-Uber
York College, York, Nebraska

Contents

Foreword

MEMOIRS DEMONSTRATE THE UNIVERSAL TRUTH THAT WE CANNOT predict the path our lives will take. And why would we want to predict the future? Some of life's best moments are serendipitous!

Betty's path has been marked by many such moments, and she openly shares them with her readers. From the tales of her unconventional Depression-era childhood to the adventures she experienced after the death of her husband, her stories have added brilliant color to the outlines that history provides.

Betty's third memoir, *Living with Twelve Men*, fills in the time gap between the first two books and weaves their stories together. She once more invites us into her life, where we share her adventures as a nineteen-year-old faculty wife in a house filled with high-spirited young men. We share her fear, joy, and confusion when she undergoes a rather harrowing introduction to parenting as a new mother more prepared for childbirth than childcare. We ride the rollercoaster of her transition into maturity, as Betty continues to fill in the blanks by introducing us to her children, weaving tales of a stable family life much different from her own childhood.

It has been my privilege not only to witness the unfolding of Betty's journey as an author but to count her among my dearest friends. When we first met in an online writing class, I was living in rural Nebraska, and she resided in California. Through the techno-magic of the Internet, along with a few phone chats, we formed a long-distance friendship. Betty's attendance at a York College reunion gave us an opportunity to meet in person, and it was as if we'd known each other since childhood.

While Betty used the online writing course as a springboard for her first memoir, *Dancing in My Nightgown*, I put writing on the back burner to concentrate on building my editing business. Our divergent paths created a fortuitous blend of abilities, and when she asked me to edit her manuscript, I jumped at the chance! Who wouldn't want to collaborate with Betty Auchard on a daily basis? Her enthusiasm is contagious, and her sense of humor is delightful.

We resumed our work together on Betty's second book, *The Home for the Friendless*, exchanging ideas in comments along the margins of the manuscript. We found humor in the comments and typos and the unlikely scenarios that came to mind, giggling our way through many of the pages like a couple of teenagers. Who said the editing process can't be fun?

Watching Betty grow from gifted storyteller to award-winning author has been an extraordinary experience. Betty's third memoir, *Living with Twelve Men*, is the book her fans (I count myself among them) have been waiting for. As Betty Auchard's path carries her into the future—one serendipitous moment at a time—I'm sure we all hope she will continue to take us along for the ride.

—Sandi Corbitt-Sears
Editor at WriteFriend.com

Pregnant with stories— the birth of a book

THIRTEEN YEARS AGO, THE SEED FOR THIS BOOK WAS PLANTED IN an email to my cousin Don. He wanted to know what it was like being a dorm mother for twelve boys in the 1950s. In the subject line of my response, I wrote, "Dorm mother has shootout on stairs." He wrote back, "Your letter really made me laugh."

I put both emails in a folder titled *Stories in Letters,* where they would be safe. Saving them seemed more important than using them at the time.

Eight years later, I enrolled in a writing class at the community center and needed an idea for my first assignment. I found the email, and that one story grew into the twenty-eight chapters you're about to read.

—Betty Auchard, 2015

Acknowledgements

THERE'S NO WAY I COULD WRITE A BOOK WITHOUT THE GUIDANCE of other people. My first readers are always my two daughters, Dodie Hively and Renee Ray. They know how much I value their input, because I tell them so all the time.

I owe a lot to two other people: Sandi Corbitt-Sears and Bruce McAllister. Sandi has been my editor since 1999. We are writing partners who love working together. Bruce has been my writing coach since 2000 and is the person who helped get my stories published.

Rev. Edward Auchard, my brother-in-law, told me the locations of Denny's ship, the Lurline, during the war. Sadly, that was our last communication, as he died three weeks later.

Jane Adams, Virginia Robinson, Jean Schneider, and Norma Jean Vorse (Mudge) provided photos and important details. It was in Ann Thompson's memoir class at the community center in Campbell, California, that I wrote the first draft. The Los Gatos Library memoir group got me through the second draft.

Barbara R. Glass, columnist and book reviewer for the *Senior Voice*, suggested adding more stories at the end about Denny, me, and our children, which we did.

University of Northern Colorado provided archival information about Union Colony and Gordon Hall.

❊

My readers:

Barbara R. Glass: Columnist and book reviewer for the *Senior Voice*.

Matilda Butler: Co-founder of WomensMemoirs.com and author of *Rosie's Daughters: The "First Woman To" Generation Tells Its Story* and *Writing Alchemy: How to Write Fast and Deep*.

Charles D. Hayes: Author of *September University: Summoning Passion for an Unfinished Life* and *A Mile North of Good and Evil*.

Chrystal Houston: Director of Alumni and Communication, York College, York, Nebraska.

Rev. Frank Medsker and Carol Medsker: York College alumni.

Lloyd Russell: Book reviewer at http://booksage.blogspot.com/

Dr. Robert Spaulding: Retired Professor of Education, San Jose State University, San Jose, California.

Dr. Benton White: Retired Professor of Religious Studies, San Jose State University, San Jose, California.

I'm always worried about leaving someone out. If you're one of those people, please forgive me. I could blame it on being eighty-five and forgetful, but I don't want everyone to know my age. I've been passing as seventy.

—Betty Auchard

Introduction

IN THE SUMMER OF 1949, A FEW YEARS AFTER V-E DAY, THE NATION was still dancing to post-war hope and a bright future for all. The country was changing, and even my family seemed more peaceful. It was almost as if the international cease-fire had prompted my parents to declare a truce. But just as peace between nations is often temporary, Mom and Dad could go back to fighting without warning.

Any discussion of politics had always created conflict between my parents. Mom voted Republican; Dad voted Democrat. When I returned from my first year of college, I noticed that they no longer argued about their opposing views. It felt odd, as if something was missing. Mom and Dad weren't fighting about *anything*, and my younger brother and sister had outgrown their orneriness. Everyone seemed a little more mature, even our dog.

My family changing for the better was practically a miracle, but I couldn't shake the feeling that something unexpected could still throw Mom into a tizzy, as it had for most of my life. Then we'd all be right back where we started, and I wanted things to stay the way they were. But that couldn't happen.

Like it or not, my reluctant plod toward adulthood had picked up speed, and the future kept whispering my name. At first I ignored it, but once it had my attention, it said, "Betty, get over your fear of growing up, or you know what'll happen?"

"No. What?"

"You won't *have* a future."

Dad helped ease my worries when he spotted an interesting editorial in the *Denver Post*. From behind the pages of the newspaper, he read aloud the last line: "Life in America is better than it's ever been." He tossed the newspaper aside and said, "Well, kids, the *Post* says our American dream has come true."

15

Maybe the newspaper was right, but if my dream of graduating from college was going to come true, I had to find a summer job so I could return to school in the fall.

※

PART I

Faculty Wife

Betty and Denny Auchard on Their Wedding Day

CHAPTER 1

Falling in Love

Not until the tenth grade did I have any interest in boys at all. Cutting off my long braids, which hung past my waist, changed that. Dad disapproved of the modern hairstyle I adopted. He said, "Cuttin' your hair means you're probably gonna change." I assured him I would always be the same girl, but I lied. The reason for cutting my hair was to change my image. It did more. It transformed my life.

The day I introduced the "new" Betty at school was the high point of my teen years. Tenth-grade guys thought I was a new student. One of them asked me out to the movies, and we went for hamburgers afterwards. Chewing and swallowing in front of a boy felt so personal that I took only a few bites. At home that night, hunger overwhelmed me, and I longed for the food I'd wasted.

Before my haircut, I'd been barely okay around boys my age. After my transformation, I became afraid of them. Those young men represented the future, and I guess I wasn't there yet. When I discovered that dating and kissing went together, it made me queasy. If a boy tried to press his lips to mine, I'd turn away and say, "I'm not ready for that."

The first teen party I ever attended almost turned me to stone. I found out fast that the craze was a version of Spin the Bottle where the boys did the bottle spinning. If the bottle pointed at a girl when it stopped, he got to kiss her whether she wanted it or not. I prayed to myself, *God, puh-leeze don't let that milk bottle stop in front of me,* but it did. My muscles stiffened instantly.

The bottle spinner looked just as scared as I felt. We went into a room where the smooching would take place and closed the door behind us. I broke the stupid rules real fast.

I said, "Look … what's your name? Rob? Well, Rob, I don't want to do this."

Rob let his breath out slowly, looking relieved. He said, "Okay, then, let's talk for a few minutes and go out smiling."

That's what we did, and the other kids assumed we'd been smooching our lips raw. I almost hugged Rob for going along with me. I probably could've shared a hamburger with him.

Spinning the bottle might have been a fun way for some people to grow up fast, but it wasn't for me. The thought of my mouth touching a boy's mouth made me feel naked. While growing up, I'd never thought about marriage either, because it seemed so far in the future that it wasn't real. Mom and Dad married and divorced each other twice and separated too many times to count. I didn't understand it. They had tried over and over to make our family normal. It was so much work that I had no intention of becoming a grown-up. Ever.

WANT IT OR NOT, ADULTHOOD CAUGHT UP WITH ME BY THE TIME I turned eighteen. I needed to find a grown-up job so I could pay for my second year of college. The want ads announced an opening at Buy-for-Less Drug Store in downtown Englewood, Colorado. I'd hoped to be the first to apply, but five girls beat me to it. During my interview, I cranked up my confidence, which led to an excited-but-scared feeling that said, "I'm ready for this … but maybe I'm not."

To my surprise, the boss hired me as head soda jerk. He said, "Betty, you're the only applicant who has gone to college," which proved that getting an education pays off.

The next thing on my summer to-do list was tanning with a mixture of baby oil and iodine, because everyone knew that a girl with a tan looked good. Looking good gave me confidence to flirt with the opposite sex, who seemed more interesting than they had before. With no embarrassment, I shared those feelings with my mother. Then I overheard her saying to Dad, "You know what, Butch? I think Betty's in heat." I decided to keep my thoughts to myself from then on.

During the years between lopping off my braids and turning eighteen, I'd practiced chewing and swallowing food during a date, but that was about it. Eventually, I started wondering how it would feel to kiss the lips that had been flopping around on a hamburger. Just because I'd been at school for nine months didn't mean I'd been necking with anyone. I still lagged behind other girls my age socially. That summer, my mind was changing itself. It seemed miraculous. I said a quiet hello to my future, because, after all, everyone has to grow up sometime. I finally accepted that I was blossoming into a young woman.

Two weeks into my job as a soda jerk, everything happened at once. I wasn't looking for a boyfriend, but I found one at a wedding rehearsal. He was the best man, and I was the wedding singer. We eyed each other while pretending to look for someone else. Almost vibrating with excitement, I became so nervous it was an effort to stand up straight and tighten my tummy. I'd read that smiling makes people look attractive, so I smiled until my face hurt. Whenever someone started a conversation with him, I grabbed the opportunity to admire his handsome profile and even his posture. He combed his wavy black hair so nicely that I couldn't stop staring.

Wait a minute ... is that gray hair I see at his temples? My heart fell. *He's too old for me.*

But I was wrong. I discovered that the fellow I was drawn to was just twenty-three, and his temples were prematurely gray. He'd served in the military and was working on a master's degree at the same college I'd been attending in Greeley. I liked him and didn't give a hoot about the five-year age difference or that he was more mature than my parents. Meeting Denny was another miracle—like my family changing for the better—and I made no effort to resist him.

I spent every week longing for the weekend to arrive. That was the only time we could be together. On Friday afternoons, he would drive fifty miles from Greeley to stay with friends so we could date and kiss and hug in his blue 1945 Dodge coupe. Every Sunday evening, he returned to Greeley to concentrate on his summer school studies. As soon as he left, I started missing him and the hours we spent in his car. I'd changed a lot in a short time, going from avoiding kissing to wanting to spend my life with a man. Passion took control of my mind, and I walked around in a daze, all dewy-eyed, distracted, and dazzled. I sensed the earth moving beneath my feet and had to admit that I'd fallen into adult love.

Denny helped me understand why kissing is so popular: it's fun! At first, I kissed with my eyes closed. Then I noticed that his were always open, so I did the same. I adored his hair and his eyes and his dark complexion and the way he smiled. It had to be love, because I liked everything about him.

We did a lot of necking and talking. I became aware of the similarities and differences between his family and mine. We both came from humble stock, though his mom and dad had gone to college. Mine dropped out of high school to find work and help support their families. His parents didn't smoke, drink, or cuss. Mine did all of that and more.

My boyfriend was reserved, a conspicuous contrast to my lively nature. I wondered how we could be so different and be so attracted to each other. I reckoned he appealed to me because of his worldly experience, while I didn't even have a driver's license. He was both handsome *and* nice, an unusual combination in a young man. He planned for the future, and I was afraid of it. I longed to be a part of his life, so I got over that fear. Then I became terrified he might get away, though I was certain he wanted me to catch him. After two months of heavy petting and deep conversations, he brought up the topic of marriage. I knew my folks would say it was too soon to take that step, but it felt right to me.

One day, Dad said, "You two are goin' out an awful lot."

My father hadn't welcomed any of the fellows I dated at Englewood High School. If their skin color differed from ours or they practiced another religion, he completely ignored them. It was humiliating. However, Dad found no fault with Denny even though he had skin darker than anyone in our family. When he asked if we'd been thinking about marriage, I said, "Yeah, Dad, we'd like to have a Thanksgiving wedding."

As I'd expected, he replied, "I can't afford it."

Denny and I had bank accounts and were prepared to pay for our own wedding. It meant I'd have to spend the money I'd saved for my sophomore year, but who cared? Not me. I felt dizzy with joy.

Our sudden decision to marry caused Mom to fret. She said, "We sure could've used your help around here with expenses."

"Ma, look at it this way ... you'll have one less mouth to feed."

"Well, then, are you pregnant?"

"No, Mom, I'm not pregnant."

My mother wrung her hands and popped tranquilizers for her nerves. I loved her, but at a very young age I had decided that anxiety was Mom's hobby. After learning I wasn't pregnant, she worried I'd go to hell for marrying outside the Missouri Synod Lutheran Church.

Dad said, "Girl, she's gonna get married. Let's thank our lucky stars she's marrying someone who's got a job." Dad's relaxed disposition balanced Mom's nervous nature.

My younger brother and sister liked Denny and were giddy with excitement at first, but knowing I'd be leaving our family put them in the dumps. Fourteen-year-old Patty asked, "What'll we do when Mom and Dad have a fight?"

"Patty, they don't fight much anymore, but if they do, just go to our bedroom and wait 'til it's over the way we've always done."

Despite my glib response, a little guilt intruded into my happiness. I knew in my heart that our parents would eventually divorce again. Bobby and Patty would have to fend for themselves after I left home.

DURING LONG CHATS WITH MY SWEETHEART, I HAD LEARNED ABOUT his job teaching math and physics at a small church college in the town of York, Nebraska. I could tell that my love had a high IQ. I'd never found out if mine was high or low, and I hoped the topic wouldn't come up. In addition to teaching and coaching football, he supervised male students in a dorm. That meant I'd be living with Denny downstairs, and twelve men would be living upstairs ... a lot of men for one house.

My curiosity led me to say, "Denny, tell me a little about our housemates. Are they tall, short, nice, or what?"

"Well, they're down-to-earth guys, Betty. You'll like them. A few are pre-med students, others plan to teach, but most of them are preparing to be ministers.

Ministers? Oh, my God.

AT THE END OF THE SUMMER, DEN RETURNED TO HIS JOBS ON THE campus in Nebraska. I wouldn't see him again until he arrived in Englewood for the ceremony that would make us man and wife. As I kissed and hugged him goodbye, I couldn't imagine how I'd get along without him for three months. I missed him and sent letters twice a week. In one of his letters to me, he ended with this note: "I miss you, and I love you. P.S. You spelled my last name wrong."

What an embarrassing mistake! To make it up to him, I sent my betrothed a shoebox filled with home-baked chocolate chip cookies so he'd know I could cook. I hoped he would compliment me. That would lift my spirits for sure.

It was a bust. The boys got to the package first, sampled the contents, and left the crumbs for him. When I found out, I went from sad to mad and back again. But that was only the beginning. Whenever I talked to my sweetheart long distance, those ministerial students eavesdropped on our lovey-dovey conversations by way of the upstairs extension line. Denny yelled, "Hang up the phone, you guys!" but they never did. I could not imagine any church in the world wanting one of them as its minister.

What would it be like with all of us in the same house? I tried not to think about it. I had a wedding to plan.

CHAPTER 2

Becoming Mrs. Auchard

To decrease wedding costs, Mom helped me make my own gown. To keep the material snowy white, we washed our hands a lot and didn't snack on anything while sewing. Taffeta is slippery, and the thought of cutting into such beautiful fabric made me so nervous that I cut my finger instead. Drops of blood landed on the bottom edge of what would become the left sleeve.

I screamed. Mom leaped from her chair and yelled, "Don't panic. I know what to do!" She grabbed the piece and dipped the edge in cold water, gently massaging the stained area before the blood could set in. Mom hadn't finished high school, but she knew a little bit about everything.

To complete my wedding ensemble, a talented neighbor created a beautiful veil as a gift. Denny and I had run out of money for the wedding and still owed twenty dollars for flowers. The universe must've been watching over us, because we found a twenty-dollar bill on the sidewalk in downtown Englewood. Another miracle! Still, becoming man and wife was expensive, costing a whopping $150.

Dad said, "Jiminy Christmas. You coulda saved all that money by eloping." A tightwad with a soft heart, Dad rarely showed his sentimental side.

On Saturday, November 26, 1949, I arrived twenty minutes late for the ceremony. Although sweaty and out of breath, I faked composure by whispering, "Betty, unwind; you can do this." I proceeded with calm demeanor and recited what I was supposed to recite and did what a bride was supposed to do. Inside, however, I was so flustered about being late to my own wedding that I longed for the ceremony to end. I found out later that the guests had grown restless, and the organist had continued to play the same welcome music long after everyone was seated. A few people thought I had dumped the groom at the last minute. If I'd known that, I would have been a wreck.

After the reception, I changed clothes and packed my belongings in two boxes. Mom noticed and asked, "Why are you taking everything you own?"

"I want my treasures with me."

Her expression revealed pure shock, and the hurt I saw in her eyes tore my heart open.

"Betty, it feels like you're running away from home."

I guess looking forward to leaving home was selfish. It was so much easier for me than my mother.

Dad broke into the awkward moment and said, "Well, you kids better get goin'."

We finished loading the car and said our goodbyes. Dad, Bob, and Patty waved while Mom wiped her eyes with a hanky. Tears that hadn't yet trickled down my cheeks sat in my eyelids, and I couldn't bear to look at her puckered face.

We drove away in silence, reflecting on the lives we'd left behind as we headed for the Brown Palace Hotel in Denver for our wedding night. I'd never slept with a man before, but I was ready to sleep with Denny.

THE NEXT MORNING, HOURS OF DRIVING TOOK US TO A CUT-RATE motel. When my sweetie apologized, I said, "I don't mind. We have to be frugal." That night we squeezed in a few hours of sleep. In the morning, we practiced making love until a maid knocked on the door. I gasped with embarrassment and a feeling of guilt. Years later, we would laugh about it, but it wasn't funny at the time. We bumped into each other, grabbing clothes while trying to dress as fast as possible. With no time to brush our teeth, we squeezed toothpaste onto our tongues and swished it around. Then we snatched up the suitcases, paid the bill, and hit the road, breathless from the rush to avoid paying for another night.

On Monday, after sailing past fields of dried cornstalks, we arrived at Thompson Hall in York by 2:00 a.m. I was totally tuckered out but eager for whatever came next.

The name Thompson Hall sounded kind of uppity, but it wasn't an uppity place. Our home, a charming, two-story, turn-of-the-century house on the corner of Kiplinger and Ninth Avenue, had a wraparound porch and a warmhearted, welcoming appearance. Nostalgia flooded through me, and I thought, *This reminds me of Grandmother's house.* Across the street, the rest of the Evangelical United Brethren campus spanned several blocks, with plenty of green grass and tall trees.

My new life started right there on the porch. Feeling silly and romantic, I said, "Husband, carry me over the threshold." When he hoisted me up, my legs got caught on the door frame, so my entry didn't quite match my dreamy expectations. *All* romantic notions fled when we reached the bedroom and Denny put me down in a hurry, saying, "What the heck ...?"

A giant-sized note on the bedroom door read, "We hid the key."

Denny said, "I didn't know we had one." He tried turning the knob and—sure enough—the door was locked.

We searched for an hour until, woozy from weariness, we found the key in the ice cube tray. I was sure the boys had hidden it there. I wanted to say, "Damn those brats," but I wasn't about to start wifehood with cussing.

At last, we gained entrance to our own private space. It boasted a large closet, a window with a pulldown shade, a rose-colored chenille bedspread, magnolia-blossom wallpaper, and ... *a sign on the ceiling?* I read it aloud. "We have wired your mattress springs to a speaker system."

"Oh, my God!"

"Betty, don't worry. The boys are just foolin' around. Believe me, they don't know how to wire anything."

Despite our hotel-room honeymoon, I was still shy, and the note on the ceiling didn't help. I was afraid to climb into bed, certain that every twitch of my toes would be broadcast through the mattress springs.

That bedroom seemed like someone else's, not mine. Despite the large closet and pretty wallpaper, it was not the private, romantic boudoir I'd created in my head. However, I smiled and laughed and kept those thoughts to myself. I would never have shared my disappointment, but I began to wonder if I was ready for marriage.

In spite of that unnerving introduction to wedded bliss, I still looked forward to life with Denny. However, marrying him and living on a church college campus meant adjusting to a more refined existence than I was used to. The drastic change wouldn't be easy, and I knew I'd miss Dad's rough-around-the-edges humor. That part of him was part of who I'd become, but Mom hated it. Whenever Dad told a slightly off-color story that made us kids snicker, it really got her goat. He defended himself by saying, "Girl, if my kids are gonna hear uncouth language, they're gonna hear it from me first."

"Why?" my mother asked.

"Why? So I can explain it to 'em."

As a new wife, I focused on one thing, to make my husband as proud of me as I was of him. If that meant giving up my rough edges, I'd have to find a way to polish myself. A year of college had helped me feel a little more adult, but marriage demanded that I behave that way all the time. What a weight to bear. I wanted to blend with the educated church folks around me, so I pretended to be smart and acted kind of holy. Anything less than smart and holy had to be cast off.

I was a nineteen-year-old housemother, and I needed to grow up fast.

York College in York, Nebraska.

CHAPTER 3

Married Too Soon?

THIS IS HOW I'D DESCRIBE YORK COLLEGE IF IT WERE FEATURED in a movie:

Millions of years after God created the earth and people, he created York College, with the help of the Evangelical United Brethren Church. The campus sits on top of a hill in York, Nebraska, closer to heaven than any structure in the county. The surroundings resemble an old master's painting, with mossy lawns, stately trees, and buildings older than our grandparents. The setting is like an 1890 movie coming to life, where Betty Auchard plays the role of the teacher's wife.

Of course, if this were a real movie review, it couldn't stop there. I'd have to introduce the young men upstairs, who spent a lot of time studying the Bible and even more time raising holy hell. They were old enough to know better but acted like sixteen-year-olds full of high jinks and monkey business.

Unfortunately, they weren't performers, paid to act ornery. They were devilish in real life, so I tiptoed around Thompson Hall, convinced that Denny's charges resented my presence. After all, my arrival had ended their free run of the place. Before I moved in, they'd cut through his apartment to reach the basement for laundry and Ping-Pong. After I arrived, they had to go outdoors and clear around to the back door to reach the basement stairs. It must've been a hassle, especially in the winter, because their door slamming sounded angry. When I mentioned it, my husband waved his hand and said, "Betty, don't worry about it. They always slam doors."

He had brushed away my complaint as though it were a fly in his face. He'd done nothing about someone hiding our bedroom key and forcing us to search for it until 3:00 a.m., when we were dog tired. He'd also ignored the alarming note on the bedroom ceiling warning that our mattress springs had been wired to a speaker system. Taken all together, it sure sent a message that said, "Colorado girl, you're an intruder." Was I supposed to laugh it off with a boys-will-be-boys attitude?

A few days later, they struck again. At least I was pretty sure it was them. One night after cleaning the kitchen, we hauled our weary bodies into bed and immediately crashed to the floor. The impact rattled my insides something awful. I pulled myself together and said, "The guys did this."

"Naw, I probably put the mattress boards on crooked."

Too tired to reassemble the frame, we slept on the mattress where it had fallen. The next morning we stumbled out of the framework. Denny looked at the mess and said, "I'll fix this later."

I wondered what human instinct makes people play tricks on each other, thinking of it as fun. I felt above that sort of nonsense until I remembered how often I used to scare the living daylights out of my little sister, Patty, in the dark. But that was different, because we were kids. The bedroom is not the place for a bride to feel angst ridden, wondering when the live-in jokesters will strike next.

I could not pretend to be okay with the boys' pranks. Someday I would seek revenge on those guys, but Denny could never know, because he was born mature and wouldn't understand.

It was easy to indulge in fantasies of retaliation, because I hadn't enrolled in classes yet and had too much time on my hands. While waiting for the new semester to begin, I accepted the job of Thompson Hall housekeeper for $3.50 a week.

Before I arrived, the upstairs residents let their part of the house get so junky and foul they had to enlist girlfriends to spiff up the place for free. I replaced the girlfriends and got paid to make everything shine. I dusted the dorm furniture, vacuumed their parlor, swept their steps, and scrubbed their bathroom. It was more work than I'd expected, but I threw myself into doing a praiseworthy job. I added the money to my savings jar, where the growing cash would eventually buy an electric mixer. Blending cookie dough with an egg beater was not so easy.

While making everything sanitary, I brooded about getting the short end of the stick. I felt my husband should've had a serious talk with the guys about the poor reception and shabby treatment they had given me. The type of pranks they pulled were not good Christian fun. But I also didn't want people to think I was whiny and delicate, so I kept those thoughts private and attempted to clean my way into everyone's hearts.

One day, while on my hands and knees scrubbing the base of the boys' toilet, a cold needle of water stung my neck. It startled the heck out of me, and I witnessed the blur of someone fleeing the crime scene. I continued with my chores and acted unruffled, as though whatever just happened was no big deal.

Remaining aloof, I stood up and sauntered down the hall past the room where the culprit lay stretched out on a cot, pretending innocence. My chance for revenge had arrived. I raced downstairs to our bedroom in search of a yellow plastic pistol I'd seen in one of Denny's drawers. I hadn't questioned why he had the toy in his possession. I found it and loaded the little tank with cold water, concealed it in my apron pocket, and lollygagged back up the stairs. The perpetrator still lay on his cot, pretending to sleep. I aimed and let him have it before escaping. His feet hit the floor in hot pursuit of me, dorm mother and invincible cleaning lady.

With the bad guy on my heels, I hugged the wallpaper on the stairwell, shooting up from below while he shot down from above. In the heat of battle, the front door opened, and Mr. Auchard, housefather and perfect role model for young men, entered the picture.

The shootout on the stairs came to an abrupt halt. In an attempt to sound amused, my husband came up with a phony laugh. I could tell he did *not* think the scene was funny. My foe returned to his cot, and Denny and I retreated to our apartment. He tugged the heavy oak sliding doors closed and leaned against them with hands behind his back. His quiet lecture took about twelve seconds.

"Betty, don't let these fellows sucker you into their shenanigans. You need to set a good example. You've gotta remember you're a faculty wife."

I felt nailed. Mom had chewed me out in a similar manner for teaching the neighbor kids how to scare their younger siblings. His reminder made me feel like a naughty child. It embarrassed and angered me, but I kept those feelings to myself. I didn't grow up disagreeing out loud with anyone, and my husband and I didn't argue, so he had no way of knowing we'd had our first conflict.

AT NINETEEN, I HADN'T LEARNED HOW TO BE GROWN UP AND DOMES-tic, although I tried. I had helped my mother with chores but always followed her lead. As a new wife, I played house, keeping the boys' areas spotless while forgetting to dust our own furniture. I bought too many groceries and couldn't freeze the extra meat, because there was barely room in our Westinghouse refrigerator for two ice cube trays. Meat turned slimy, and vegetables rotted before I could use them.

The wedding gift of a Pyrex percolator encouraged us to become coffee drinkers. I followed the instructions that came with the box and made a full pot and reheated the leftover brew every morning. By the third day, Denny noticed an odd grayish color after adding milk. He took a sip and said, "This tastes *awful*."

I said, "Maybe it has gone over." That's what my parents said whenever milk soured. My three-day-old coffee had probably gone over. I had a lot to learn.

Denny's white shirts challenged my ability to do laundry on my own. After washing them, I rinsed the shirts in too much bluing before dunking them in starch thick as glue. After leaving the laundry on the clothesline until everything dried, I dampened the stiff-as-cardboard garments and rolled them in a towel for a few hours so they'd be just right for ironing. I usually waited too long, and mildew grew until the white fabric turned into a light blue science project. The same thing had happened at home, but Mom helped me start over. With her living in Colorado and me in Nebraska, I bleached the bloody life out of the mildewed shirts with no guidance, which made my husband smell like a swimming pool whenever he wore a white shirt.

I was an expert at ironing but an amateur at starching. My mother had done that job, too. I used more than necessary, causing garments to stand on their own. My husband had to pry his hands into each sleeve to crack it open. Buttoning the stiff shirts required strength and dexterity. When he finally made his way inside a starched shirt, he looked kind of crispy.

My sister-in-law, Glenna, and her husband, Carl, lived across the street. They'd been married a whole year, so she knew all about laundry. Glenna taught me how to add the right amount of bluing and starch. It was one of the reasons we became best friends. The other reason? I liked her.

❧

AS A HOUSEMOTHER TO TWELVE MALE STUDENTS, I NEEDED TO ACT AS mature as their housefather, but it didn't feel natural. I wondered if it ever would. It so confused and frustrated me that I had a bad dream. I was wearing a white dress and veil while walking down the aisle toward Denny and recognized a nice lookin' young man in the congregation. It caused me to gasp and clutch my breast the way women did in the movies. He gazed at me with sorrowful eyes and then raised his hand and waved as if saying, "So long, Betty." It was Johnnie Evans, my first boyfriend from high school. I woke up sad, thinking, *Have I married too soon?*

CHAPTER 4

Forbidden Fun

SOON AFTER ARRIVING AT THOMPSON HALL, OUR FIRST RESIDENCE as wide-eyed newlyweds, I learned what Denny already knew: the rules at York College were strict. Worse, they included a prohibition on dancing.

In high school, before I ever met my future husband, I got chummy with other girls who didn't have boyfriends. I joined them for every dance held in the gymnasium, even though my church didn't allow dancing. Many of us didn't know the difference between a boogie-woogie and a rumba. We attended just to hang out and socialize.

Sitting on the sidelines week after week, I found myself doing less talking and more watching as other kids bounced to the beat of the band. I found myself tapping my toes and swaying, no matter how immoral it might be. I liked the ambiance of a ballroom, the inviting rhythms, the happy couples, and the buoyant mood. I longed to join everyone out there instead of huddling around the edges of the basketball court yelling conversations over loud music. I yearned for the freedom to swing and sway as the melody commanded. If I had to answer to anyone for my unholy behavior, I would say, "It's not my fault. The music made me do it." Music and movement were as natural as bread and butter; they were meant for each other.

Why couldn't we have found a dancing church instead of the church Mom forced us to attend?

When I went away for my first year of college, the temptation to boogie was even greater, because I was fifty miles from home. With no guilt at all, I broke my church's rules and showed up at parties with the intention of participating in the sacrilegious act of dancing. Now *that* was what I called heaven. I wanted to attend every scheduled event where students gyrated to a lively beat or sailed across the room during a waltz.

And then I met Denny, as had been divinely appointed. Every weekend during the summer of 1949, we whirled about the ballroom to the magical rhythms of Eddie Howard's band at the famous Elitch Gardens pavilion in Denver. My sweetheart and I connected in a new way, temporarily abandoning our former selves.

Dancing was more spiritual than anything I'd ever experienced. Music told my body what to do, which prompted a spine-tingling communication between soul and sound. If I discovered something that wonderful so late in life, what other miracles could be out there for this nineteen-year-old?

One evening, as my sweetheart and I spun across the room, waving our arms and wiggling our hips to the tempo, a man tapped Denny's shoulder. He leaned in and said, "Folks, please leave the dance floor so I can speak with you."

His next words were puzzling. "No breaking is allowed here."

"What do you mean by breaking?" I asked.

"When you move apart from each other, it's called breaking."

"I thought we were doing the jitterbug."

The man frowned at me, obviously interpreting my confusion as sarcasm.

We got used to ballroom etiquette real fast at Elitch Gardens that summer.

Once we moved to the York College campus, we had to leave our ballroom education behind because there would never be a dance we could attend. I focused instead on the compulsory activities, which involved alphabetical seating in daily chapel to make it easy for those in charge to monitor attendance. I showed up on time and bowed my head with everyone else, but I wasn't thinking about God. I was writing my grocery list. I'd scribble *canned tuna, mushroom soup,* and *noodles* in time to say "amen" before rushing off to the mandatory class I'd nicknamed "Bible for Beginners."

In addition to my religious obligations, I jumped into my nonspiritual duties as housemother/faculty wife/new student. I had no clue that a lot of the girls on campus were dying to find out what I was like until my sister-in-law Glenna dropped that piece of news into a conversation. I asked why. She said, "They think of you as competition."

"Competition for what?"

"They want to see what you have that they don't have."

"Why would they care?"

"They care because most of them had crushes on your hubby."

That worried me. Those envious girls could easily discover my worldly side, which wasn't up to York College standards. I feared I wouldn't fit in as a faculty wife, and I didn't want the real Betty to hurt Denny's reputation. He was an athlete and a college leader. Even the downtown merchants admired him—and I shared the spotlight. But acting mature and holy was wearing me out.

Then something happened that lightened my attitude. It started when my husband announced, "Guess what? I've got a moonlighting job."

"Really? Doing what?"

"I'll referee for out-of-town football games."

"Have you ever done that before?"

"Betty, I'm the assistant football coach, remember?"

"Oh, that's right."

"I'll get fifteen dollars a game. This means we can do some things we couldn't afford before."

With a twinkle in his eye, he added, "I took this out-of-town job to get away from my real job on campus once in a while."

His response caught me off guard. I had no idea he was feeling as held down as I was. Thank heaven the man I met in Colorado still existed. After we married, I began to believe that he lived through the eyes of others, even if he wasn't aware of it. I'd been shocked when I learned how far he'd gone to make his mom and dad happy after the death of his older brother, Lester, during the last four months of the war.

Lester's death had sent his parents reeling. Among the five children, Lester had been the golden boy and was admired by all. He had been married only nine months when a message arrived saying that his submarine, the USS Lagarto, had been declared missing. The military gave Denny an honorable discharge so he could return home to care for his distraught parents. They were so filled with despair he would've done anything to make them smile.

The perfect opportunity resided in their home. Their new boarder, Bonnie, taught sixth graders at the local school. Den's parents had grown fond of her and thought of her as a family member, and my sweetie jumped at the chance to please them by dating her. That thrilled his mother, and the color returned to her cheeks. After he gave the pretty teacher an engagement ring, his dad also beamed with pleasure. Oh, happy day for three people: Mother, Father, and Bonnie.

What about Denny? He soon realized his mistake and resolved to discover some affection for Bonnie by smooching. Except for several gentle kisses, they hadn't really "necked," as most lovers do. Surely, if he practiced as often as possible, he could develop some excitement for her, so they hugged and kissed quite a lot. It worked for Bonnie, and she often had to wipe her sweaty brow and say, "Oh, my …" The more they necked, the more excited she got and the more frustrated he became. It wasn't happening the way he'd planned, and Denny grew anxious and depressed. Then warts started growing on his neck, making it hard to shave. The family doctor said warts could be caused by worry. Well, he was worried sick that he might never learn how to love Bonnie. He finally broke off the relationship, and his parents were twice as sad as before.

Denny told me the story when we started dating two years later to explain the bumps on his neck, which still interfered with shaving. The doctor had said, "When the source of your anxiety is behind you, those things will eventually stop growing." A few months after we married, they completely disappeared. I felt special. Marrying me had cured him of warts.

No one would ever understand what that did for my ego.

THE EVENING WE DROVE TO HIS FIRST MOONLIGHTING JOB IN HASTINGS, Nebraska, I thought about how different Denny seemed since we moved to York. I had begun to wonder why I'd been attracted to such a buttoned-up guy. While teaching and living with students, my husband projected a sober, serious side. When he wasn't under scrutiny, he transformed back into the relaxed and fun guy I'd fallen in love with. I was so relieved.

That night, I discovered even more about his adventurous side. It was all because we had trouble finding a parking place. The whole town had turned out to support the Broncos, and it took us a while to locate an empty slot two blocks from the campus. After setting the brake and removing the keys, he said, "Hey, look where we've landed."

"What do you mean?"

"Look at what's in front of us."

"You mean this place called Larry's Liquors?"

"Yeah. Betty, do you know what I'm thinking?"

"I *think* I know what you're thinking."

We had talked about buying wine someday to remind us of a memorable date at the Blue Parrot Inn in Denver. Drinking a glass of merlot with a gourmet dinner made us feel sophisticated. Then the dessert of ice cream drizzled with wine sauce gave us a happy glow. After Denny paid the bill and tipped the waiter, contentment spread over us like a warm blanket. Of course, it's possible we'd just gotten tipsy. Whatever it was, we wanted to experience it again. But the campus no-imbibing rule regarding alcoholic beverages kept us from even cooking with wine. We had no idea how or where we could purchase a bottle until finding that parking place in front of Larry's Liquors. That's when I realized Denny had decided to buy our forbidden fruit juice right there in Hastings, sixty-one miles from York, where no one knew us but God.

We didn't know how to shop in a liquor store and were baffled by all the options. Denny kept his lips from moving as he muttered, "Act natural, like we're studying the selections."

"Will do." My lips didn't move either. I was faking when I said "will do," wanting him to feel comfortable. I had no more idea than he did what to buy.

My dad bought lots of dark red wine, so I thought it was the only color available. Being surrounded by bottles filled with numerous shades of liquid overwhelmed me. Confusion reigned until I spied a glitzy container with a grapevine pattern molded into the glass. I said, "I love this bottle."

Denny said, "What's inside is pretty, too."

The gold label revealed the name: Manischewitz. Everything about it looked elegant. We bought a bottle and hid it under a blanket in the trunk of our car. Learning how to add the forbidden liquid to recipes seemed exciting. I was eager to get back to York and talk to his sister, Glenna, a superb cook. She probably knew all about the subject. We would invite her and Carl to be guests at our first gourmet meal.

Our plan thrilled me, mostly because Denny and I had connected again. I found it hard to believe my reserved husband had purchased a beverage he had to hide under a blanket in the car and then conceal behind the milk in our refrigerator at home. What an eye-opener.

We were living on the edge.

PART 2

Keeping Secrets

Francis and Elizabeth Auchard

CHAPTER 5

The Auchards

I TRIED NOT TO BE NERVOUS, BUT IF I THOUGHT ABOUT IT TOO MUCH, nervous is what I would be. I'd met my in-laws twice, but I'd never stayed overnight with them. This time, Denny's parents, Reverend Frances Auchard and his wife, Elizabeth, wanted their congregation to meet their new daughter-in-law, so Carl, Glenna, Denny, and I had decided to spend the weekend with them.

I'd never encountered such God-centered people as Denny's parents. *Earthy* best described me. I knew I would have to edit my thoughts before opening my mouth. Being myself could make me seem unrefined, so I decided not to be myself while visiting them.

Before we left home, Denny made me even more anxious by saying, "Betty, you're chatty, so you'll have to be especially careful what you say around my folks. Never suggest we go to the movies if it's Sunday … and don't ever bring up the subject of liquor."

"Why not?"

"Doncha remember the story I told you?"

"Oh, yeah, *that* story."

He had told me the true tale of a stranger who had attended Reverend Auchard's church one Sunday just to check out the preacher who might become his adversary. The man was so caught up in Dad Auchard's rousing sermon that he went forward during the altar call and got himself saved. Getting saved meant giving up a lot of sinful stuff, like making and drinking booze. That former sinner turned out to be the local bootlegger. Churchgoers viewed his salvation as a victory, while drinkers considered it a disaster. Thirsty folks in the county wanted to know why that terrible thing happened and who caused it. In no time at all, word spread that Reverend Auchard's sermon had turned the man around. Their favorite bootlegger had converted into an anti-alcohol guy, and the drinkers sought revenge. Life became scary for the Auchards when gunshots shattered their windows and a rattlesnake took up residence in the mailbox. Denny remembered it well, and he feared the subject of wine would revive bad memories for his parents.

While we visited the religious folks in Kansas, our Manischewitz would remain hidden in the refrigerator at home. It worried me, because keeping secrets had a strange effect on my common sense. Despite Denny's warning, I might start laughing about something else and blurt out, "We're hiding booze in the refrigerator!" I started chanting a protective mantra: *don't mention wine don't mention wine don't mention wine.*

MY CHURCHIFIED IN-LAWS HAD MET IN SEMINARY. THEY HAD PLANNED to serve God as missionaries in a foreign country as soon as Frances completed his training. Then a mastoid infection, which left him ill for months and destroyed the hearing in his left ear, forced him to drop out of school and return to his family's 400-acre farm to earn a living. It was not the life they'd planned. Eventually, he finished his theological training by way of a readers' course and became a pastor in rural communities in Kansas. Elizabeth believed her dream of being a missionary had finally come true. She didn't mind trading Africa for Kansas, because chickens and cows were safer than elephants and water buffalos.

Reverend Auchard's talent for revitalizing rural congregations that needed transfusions meant that Frances, Elizabeth, and their five children relocated every three years.

Frances had the gift of gab. His wife did not. Elizabeth, who was more scholarly, soft spoken, patient, and refined had read the entire Bible twelve times, underlining favorite passages during each reading. If a church member shared worries with the preacher's wife, she came up with scripture that calmed the spirit and soothed the soul.

Elizabeth seldom spoke up in public unless addressed, and she stayed close by her husband's side for a reason. When someone addressed Frances, he always replied, "What?" because he couldn't hear out of his left ear. Elizabeth jumped in immediately to act as interpreter.

Mother and Dad Auchard followed a daily ritual. After a country breakfast of bacon, eggs, fried potatoes, biscuits, and coffee, they cleared the dishes and commenced with their morning devotions. He always kept the Bible and a copy of the *Upper Room,* a devotional guide, close at hand. On my first visit, he read the lesson for the day and picked Glenna to read the scripture. After the reading, he raised his palms to the air and said, "Let us pray."

I bowed my head, but the others stood up as if to leave. I got close to Denny and asked, "What's happening?" He pressed a finger to his lips and kneeled by his chair. When everyone else kneeled, too, I followed their example. *Let's see … place my elbows on the seat, bow my head, and shut my eyes tight. Okay. I'm ready.*

Dad Auchard started the prayer chain, and my new relatives each took a turn. While on my knees, I learned a lot about Denny's family. They talked to God about a variety of subjects, such as whatever had been vexing them. Glenna thanked God for a passing grade in physics, and Denny thanked God for the moonlighting job that would make life easier for us. Their prayers came so naturally that I got lost in their joys and sorrows. Then everyone grew quiet. Was it my turn? Oh, my God, it was. I had no prayerful thoughts and said quietly, "I pass."

It sounded like I was playing poker, but I didn't know what else to do. I'd never said a prayer in front of people. Later, while Carl and I dried the dishes, he whispered, "I pass? You had a bad hand?" We squeezed back giggles so hard that tears came. Carl wiped his eyes with the dish towel and said, "Don't worry, Betty. It takes practice to pray out loud." Carl wasn't kidding. But I was an Auchard now, so I had to start talkin' to God in public.

During our first weekend with my in-laws, church members delivered homegrown vegetables, freshly baked bread, real cream, fat strawberries, angel food cake, delicious casseroles, and two just-killed chickens. The good eats reminded me of the wine we'd purchased. Thank goodness only my husband was nearby when I blurted out, "Denny, I'll bet Glenna knows how to cook with wine. Let's ask her."

Denny's wrinkled frown meant *shush*. My mantra had failed me.

CHAPTER 6

Measuring Up

DURING OUR VISIT TO KANSAS, WE NEVER SEEMED TO STOP EATING, drinking, and congregating in the kitchen, where everyone helped with whatever had to be done. Denny and I were assigned chicken duty. The two dead birds appeared to be bare naked but were still wearing little feathers. So creepy. It reminded me of the summer Dad had raised a flock in our backyard in order to put food on the table. We kids had named them. After killing Lucy, Dad had expected us to eat her. I watched in horror while the rest of the family devoured our former pet. It made me wonder if the birds we were about to dissect had names.

I shook off the bad memory to listen to Denny's instructions about plucking the creatures and scorching the fuzz off their carcasses with a lighted match. Gradually, I got caught up in the preparation and forgot all about poultry as pets.

"Wow. This is fun. What happens next?"

Denny pulled a knife from a drawer and explained. "First, we hone the blade so it will cut through the flesh like butter."

"Hone?"

He demonstrated by pulling each side of the blade across a stone, which made a sound that set my teeth on edge. Then he tested the blade by scraping it across his thumbnail, which meant that *hone* must be a fancy word for *sharpen*. The words my husband used always impressed me so much that I knew our kids would grow up with great vocabularies.

49

"Okay, what's next?"

Denny's family gathered around to watch the demonstration, and we stood in the middle of the huddle. He said, "Piece by piece, I'll show you how to separate this bird into its familiar parts: drumsticks, thighs, wings, and breast." Grabbing one of the legs, he twisted it to show how it attached to the carcass.

When he handed me the sharpened knife, I cut through the flesh at the hip, expecting the leg to come off, but it just flopped around. I asked, "How do you unhook this thing?"

"By breaking the hip joint."

"Eeew. Breaking it? Why can't we cut this piece off instead?"

"It's hard to cut through gristle and cartilage. Why don't you want to break it?"

"Well, it seems that I'm hurting something."

"The chicken can't feel it."

How could I explain to my husband that *I* would feel it?

He described how to hold the body down while twisting and turning the joint until it broke. To show his family their son had not married a delicate city girl, I took a deep breath, wrestled that limb, and ripped it off the carcass with brute force. The experience was a mix of pleasure and horror.

Denny said, "Perfect. Now find the joint between the drumstick and thigh and separate them."

I felt a little nervous but shook it off and focused on my next task, which meant making a few cuts and breaking something again. Easy as pie. I stood with a drumstick in one hand and a thigh in the other, as proud as if I'd climbed Mt. Everest. My in-laws applauded.

Our butchering job had barely begun when Carl and Glenna insisted on showing me a different method. While trying out their technique, I sliced my knuckle, which bled all over the other chicken leg. Dad Auchard stepped in, bandaged my injury, and reassigned me to whipping cream duty.

My experience with whipping cream was limited, because families as poor as mine never bought things like that. I had to trust my judgment, assuming the more you beat it, the fluffier it became. That's what happened with mashed potatoes. But I was so wrong. Instead of trusting my judgment, I should have asked before cranking the dial on the Sunbeam mixer up to eight. When the cream clumped a little, I pushed the dial to nine, which I assumed would surely turn the lumps into puffy, smooth peaks, but, instead, they got clumpier. It made me frantic. Inside my head, I screamed, *What the hell's happening?* Dad Auchard checked on my progress, and his shoulders slumped in disappointment when he saw yellow lumps instead of fluffy, white peaks.

Mother Auchard, patient soul, said, "This is the perfect time for Betty to learn how to make butter." She pushed the mixer to level ten and beat the heck out of the stuff until it turned stiff. Butter formed before my eyes. She asked, "Betty, shall we salt it or not?"

"You put salt in butter?"

Dad Auchard's shoulders sagged even lower. I could tell his taste buds were dreaming about strawberries and whipped cream on top of angel food cake. He showed no enthusiasm for my butter lesson. What a humbling experience. He just said, "Betty, when you're finished, maybe you and Denny could set the table."

We had been banished from the kitchen. Denny told me not to worry, but it didn't help. A wife should know way more than I did when we married. If the rest of his family noticed my obvious lack of experience in running a household, they kept it to themselves. Would Denny ever feel proud of me the way I was, instead of the way I should be?

In spite of my blunder, supper tasted superb. We enjoyed crusty fried chicken, sliced vine-ripened tomatoes, cucumber salad, freshly picked asparagus, and homemade bread spread with *my* homemade butter. With so much food stuffed into our bellies, no one missed dessert. Tapping my spoon against a water glass caused everyone to look up. I said, "I want to give an after-dinner blessing." Bowing my head, I closed my eyes, and said, "Thank you, God, for making us too full to miss angel food cake with strawberries and whipped cream. Amen."

Praying my first out-loud prayer felt pretty good.

ON SUNDAY MORNING, WE ROSE EARLY FOR THE CHURCH SERVICE NEXT door. Denny's parents greeted worshipers as they arrived, and people hugged and laughed so loud you would've thought it was Saturday. The women looked spiffy in their Sunday hats, probably ordered from the Sears & Roebuck catalog. Mom and Dad shopped there, too. Without their work hats, farmers revealed white foreheads and sunburned ears. Children hustled off to Sunday school classes, while adults found their favorite pews and settled in.

Dad Auchard had saved the front row for us. I sat up straight and paid attention, sensing that the congregation was looking me over to see if I measured up. If I didn't live up to their expectations, news would travel fast on telephone party lines, so I sat even taller and put on my church face. It almost felt natural.

After announcements, singing, Bible reading, and pledge gathering came the main feature, the sermon. Reverend Auchard talked with his whole body, his arms flailing the air and his voice rising and falling as he emphasized each point. My eyes were glued to the pulpit, and my ears took in every word. He pleaded, "Folks, keep God in your lives. We are nothin' without the Lord. Nothin'." The congregation agreed with soft sounds like "mhm." When they were really stirred up, they shouted, "Yes, Lord!" or "Aymen, brother!" My father-in-law sure could keep an audience awake. Mother Auchard paid close attention and wrote in a tablet as he spoke. Denny had told me that his father always asked his mother's opinion regarding the sermon. Taking notes helped her remember the details they would discuss later.

After the last hymn and the benediction, Reverend Auchard raised his hands and said, "Now you folks go in peace, and I'll see ya at the evenin' service."

The evening service? I tried to look nonchalant, as if attendance at evening services was a weekly occurrence.

People tore off in pickup trucks and old cars while we meandered across the lawn to the manse, munched on leftovers, and flopped onto the living room rug for an afternoon of rest. Frances and Elizabeth sat in their overstuffed chairs and closed their eyes while the rest of us stretched out on the rug to read the Sunday paper. Peacefulness and a sense of belonging settled over me. If it had been any other day, we would've played cards or gone to the movies, but never on Sunday.

After reading the paper, we all fell asleep. Taking a nap on the floor was heaven. When the time came for the evening service, all of us tidied our clothes, finished off the leftovers, and hustled back for more singing, praying, and chatting. Before saying farewell, our new friends made us promise to come back soon. It surprised me that church could be so much fun, and I looked forward to returning.

After hugging my in-laws goodbye, I climbed into the back of our 1947 two-door Dodge coupe beside Glenna for the long drive back to York. Darkness and quiet settled over us as the guys yakked on and on about football. The perfect time had arrived to ask Glenna an important question. I tapped her knee and said, "Glenna, I hope you've cooked with wine, because Denny and I bought some while we were in Hastings. I'm dying to try it out. Glenna?"

She had fallen asleep.

Glenna and Carl Bott

CHAPTER 7

Coming Clean

MY DAD LIKED TAKING LONG SUNDAY DRIVES TO VISIT OUT-OF-TOWN aunts and uncles. We kids piled into our assigned spots in the backseat, while my parents took their places in the front. After a full day of laughing, eating, and playing with cousins, we were usually too pooped to talk on the long drive home. Falling asleep in the silent car felt as peaceful as a sweet dream. When Dad slowed down and turned off the motor, Mom always said in a singsong voice, "We're home!" That's when we knew our pleasant journey had ended.

Riding in the car that night with Carl, Glenna, and Denny reminded me of those family outings. As I listened to the soft sounds of my sister-in-law dozing beside me, I eavesdropped on the guys' conversation about their memories of playing college football. Carl said, "Auch, remember that lucky catch in Wayne State's territory when you ran all the way back for a touchdown?"

Denny said, "Do you remember when the trainer cut the tape from my ribs and sliced my skin instead of the tape?"

"I damn sure do. How many stitches was that?"

"Twelve. I've got the scar to prove it." My husband never used swear words, even if someone cussed in his presence.

Glenna woke up and asked, "Betty, is there a blanket in the car?"

"Nope. We have one in the trunk, though. We use it to cover things up."

"What kinda things?"

"Um ... things we don't want people to see." The reminder of the bottle we'd hidden under that blanket prompted me to ask, "Do you know how to cook with wine?"

"Heavens no; I wouldn't have that stuff in the house."

SOON AFTER WE RETURNED HOME, THE SECOND SEMESTER STARTED, and I officially enrolled as a sophomore. It felt good to be back in school, but no one knew the real me, since that person hadn't shown up yet. I was still finding out what made the new Betty Auchard tick. Because I knew how to blend, everyone accepted me, assuming we had religion in common. I believed in God and prayed, though I wasn't religious.

Attending catechism class in our family church had planted a seed of skepticism about religion. It didn't help my attitude when the minister refused to perform my wedding ceremony, saying, "Your betrothed is not a member of our faith." He then suggested that my fiancé join our church. When I replied that he had his own in Nebraska, the reverend just looked at the ceiling. I followed his gaze, wondering what he saw up there, and said, "Reverend, we *will* get married, so I'll find someone else to help us out."

He sighed and said, "Hold your horses. I'll perform the ceremony on one condition."

"What's the condition?"

"You must promise to do all you can to convert your husband to our faith."

Out loud, I said, "Okeydokey." Inwardly, I thought, *Reverend, two can play this blackmail game. My fingers are crossed.*

After negotiating with our pastor, that house of worship seemed like an auction house where you had to bargain for what you wanted. I had bid on Denny and won.

GIVEN MY UNCERTAINTY ABOUT CHRISTIANITY, LIVING ON AN Evangelical United Brethren college campus didn't feel natural. Taking part in their mission to boost enrollment wasn't natural either, but the time had come to put my doubts aside and shine by doing what suited me best.

I loved acting and had always dreamed of being in the movies. I'd practiced by giving plays on our porch with the neighbor kids, and it was just as much fun as going to a matinee. In high school, I joined the Thespian Society. I also sang whenever I could. Now I would sing with the York College traveling choir, which performed in churches to draft students between Nebraska and California during spring break.

My personal beliefs didn't interfere with my singing, and I figured I might even learn something new. I had achieved perfect attendance in daily chapel and received high grades in *religion* class, for God's sake. And surprise, surprise: reading the Bible was interesting. A lot of incredible stuff happened back then.

Developing an interest in the Good Book wasn't the only surprise. It still astounded me that before my arrival, many girls on that Christian campus had lusted after my husband. Those holy hussies didn't appreciate having the object of their affection marry an out-of-state girl.

A new friend said, "Betty, I hate to admit it, but when word got around that Auch was bringing a wife to campus, I despised you."

"You did?"

"Yeah, before meeting you."

"Why?"

"I'm a former Denny stalker."

"A Denny stalker?"

"We gave ourselves that name. A lot of us are still out there."

Jiminy Christmas! What a shock.

From then on, I tried to be nice to every girl who talked to me. Widespread crushes on my husband didn't make me nervous; they flattered me. His gentle manners and dark good looks could not be ignored. Personally, I thought he could loosen up a little, though his quiet intelligence proved to be part of his appeal and made him an asset to the college. The administration wanted Denny to take over as recruiter on the next year's choir trip. Dr. Savery, a religion professor and Evangelical United Brethren pastor with a British accent, had held the position for a long time, and he planned to retire.

A small, white-haired fellow with a teensy mustache that curled up at the tips, Dr. Savery attracted young people, who viewed him as an intellectual curiosity. His novel appearance had helped him enlist a modest number of students for the college. The administration hoped my husband could attract a broader selection of students. His athletic skills caused boys to look up to him, and the fact that he taught science and math triggered respect from the brainy kids on campus. His handsome face meant girls signed up for his classes no matter what he taught. Denny ranked highly with York College students.

While my husband and I looked forward to traveling together with the choir the following year, my schedule that year kept me busy with extra rehearsals. It was my first concert tour, and I'd never done anything like it. Denny and I would be apart for two weeks.

⚜

DURING ANY AVAILABLE FREE TIME, DENNY, CARL, GLENNA, AND I played Canasta or meandered into town to window-shop, where everything we "bought" cost nothing. It was the only kind of shopping we could afford. Even though we didn't pay rent or utilities in the dorm, our yearly wage of $2,500 barely covered expenses. On Fridays, we pooled leftovers and invented unusual casseroles. Sometimes we ate them. During one of those do-it-yourself dinners, I said, "Hey, everyone. I want to cook a gourmet meal for us."

Carl asked, "What will make it gourmet?"

"Wine."

Glenna's eyebrows rose. "You bought wine?"

"Yep."

"Betty, where did you buy it?"

"At a special place in Hastings." I felt like an undercover beverage buyer.

"You drove all the way to Hastings to buy ... *alcohol*?"

Her big brother jumped in and said, "Gee whiz, sis; we're not talking about opium."

With our secret in the open, our guests sat in stunned silence. Denny's comment revealed that he and I had joined forces in a clandestine activity. I was so proud of him.

Goodbye Kiss

CHAPTER 8

Wine-Soaked Dinner

MY SWEET, BROAD-MINDED HUSBAND CONVINCED HIS SISTER AND brother-in-law that owning an alcoholic beverage didn't count as a sin. After all, if Jesus turned water into wine for a huge crowd, they probably drank it.

With that issue behind us, we scheduled a dinner date for the following Sunday. I could hardly wait to play chef. The week seemed a month long. Finally, the time came to arrange the pot roast, potatoes, carrots, and onions in the electric roaster before leaving for church. The food would be almost ready when we returned

I felt inspired while singing hymns but daydreamed during the sermon and prayers. My thoughts kept drifting to the special dinner awaiting us at home and the wine lurking in the refrigerator. How many people in the congregation would be shocked if they knew what we were hiding, and how many of them enjoyed an occasional drink without guilt? Did they care if anyone found out? Would I ever stop feeling guilty?

Hiding our activities seemed necessary, because if someone important decided a faculty member wasn't living up to York College standards, it could lead to chastisement or even termination. I prayed no one would learn about our dinner with an alcoholic beverage as the featured ingredient.

When the church service ended, the four of us zoomed home and straight to the kitchen, where we could "sin" in privacy. Oh, joy! Our apartment smelled as good as Auntie Marge's Uptown Village Tavern, where Dad tended bar and Mom did the cooking. I practically grew up there. Most of Auntie Marge's customers attended church, and they didn't view drinking beer now and then as shameful.

Denny set the table and encouraged our guests to enjoy the meal without guilt. I felt cultured, on a mission to change the attitude of my sister-in-law and her husband.

Half an hour before sitting down to eat, I set the bottle free from its prison behind the milk, baptized the roast with one cup of Manischewitz, and replaced the cover on the electric roaster. I performed those tasks as though they were old hat, even when I didn't know what I was doing. Pretending to be an expert gave me courage.

Carl watched my every move. When I set the timer for thirty minutes, he asked, "What's happening now?"

"I'm letting the wine marry the flavors of meat and vegetables."

"Marry the food?"

"Yeah, marry the food."

That was the way chefs talked. I'd seen it in the movies.

After the timer announced that our feast was ready, I sliced chunks of pot roast and dished food onto each plate. Then I spooned red juice from the bottom of the pan over the meat and vegetables and placed each serving on the table. Once plated, the tempting portions resembled photos from my *Better Homes and Gardens* cookbook. I felt so puffed up with pride that I was about to burst.

The first bite shocked my mouth and made my eyes water. The marriage of flavors had failed; it tasted like meat and vegetables with wine poured on top, with no resemblance to the food at the fancy restaurant. Even so, I chomped every bite with enthusiasm, trying to convince myself that we were eating a gourmet meal. Glenna chewed thoughtfully before saying through a mouthful of alcohol-soaked potatoes, "Interesting."

I had hoped for more. "Exotic, isn't it?" I asked. The word *exotic* sounded appropriate.

Denny suddenly stood up. Through tight lips, he said, "Scuse me" and disappeared into the bathroom. Carl and Glenna ate just enough to be supportive and not enough to get sick. It was clear that my special meal hadn't gone as planned. Hoping to save face, I said, "You'll love dessert!"

"Dessert?" Carl looked panic stricken.

On our date at the Blue Parrot Inn in Denver, we'd ordered a dessert with a French name, *Glace avec Sauce Vin,* and hadn't really appreciated it. We concluded that our taste buds were unsophisticated, just as Carl and Glenna's were.

I scooped vanilla ice cream into small bowls, dribbled Manischewitz on top, and christened each serving with a maraschino cherry, hoping the extra touch might save the day. The cherry on top was not what caught our attention. The wine soon curdled the ice cream, which created a concoction resembling baby spit up. Glenna placed a dainty bite on her tongue, held it there for a few seconds, and said, "No thanks."

Denny said, "This is nothing like the dessert in Denver."

I said, "It's very close."

What a lie. I'd never eaten anything that strange before, but I swallowed every bite, pretending it was yummy. I had something to prove.

Carl said, "Let's see what it's like straight from the bottle."

Maybe Carl would give our dinner a happy ending, though his suggestion shocked me. I had the notion that someone connected to York College would never drink wine. He poured the pretty liquid into little plastic juice glasses, giving each of us about two tablespoons. We took our time sipping it and agreed it tasted pretty good by itself.

Denny suggested a toast. After we clunked our glasses together, he said, "We should've done this in the first place."

Finally free of all pretenses, I joined the group as we sipped our Manischewitz. We indulged in a second round and became kind of giggly. My tongue felt fat when I said, "We bear quit 'fore someone knocks onna door 'n turns us in." I put the cork in place and returned the bottle to the safety of the fridge. While shoving it behind the milk, I thought, *My dad woulda laughed at this, because he always kept his jug in plain sight where he could reach it.*

⁂

The pretty bottle stayed hidden in the refrigerator. By spring break, the subject rarely came up, but we never forgot about the leftover wine stashed behind the milk.

Carl, Glenna, and I had to start packing to leave for two weeks of singing and recruiting students throughout the western states. On the day we were scheduled to depart, a crowd gathered around the bus as family members arrived to hug and kiss their loved ones goodbye. Our kiss lasted much longer than the ones other guys planted on their girls.

Our driver packed luggage into the basement of the bus, and choir members climbed aboard. The driver asked over his shoulder, "Dr. Savery, is everyone here?"

"Indeed they are, so let's push off."

The driver said, "Okay, let's roll."

When the bus pulled away, I stuck my head out the window and yelled to my husband, "You'll be coming with us next year!" He waved back, and I kept my eyes on him for a long time as he got smaller and smaller in the distance. We turned a corner, and he disappeared.

Sadness and worry settled over me. I leaned back in the seat, thinking, *We're leaving Denny alone with an alcoholic beverage in the fridge. When he's teaching a class, what if one of the boys decides to borrow our milk?*

⁂

Chapter 9

The Problem with Secrets

I'D BEEN A WIFE FOR ONLY FIVE MONTHS WHEN I LEFT MY HUSBAND at home to go on tour with the choir. Our purpose, recruiting students for the college, meant singing with the voices of angels. Grueling practice sessions demanded energy we had to fake. Jimmy Koontz, our director, said, "If you show up with dark circles under your eyes, you haven't taken care of yourself." When one of us caught a cold, he had no sympathy. He said, "You singers have an obligation to stay well."

I admired him and his high standards, even though he was uncompromising about good health. I thought I was doing everything right, but I was wrong. One day I simply cleared my throat, prompting a lecture to the whole group.

"Never clear your throat as Betty just did. You're not getting rid of phlegm; you're tossing it around."

I coughed and asked, "How do I sing with that stuff in there?"

"Sing through it or fake it, but don't clear your throat. It's hard on your vocal cords."

Performing with the York College Choir was an honor, so I paid attention to everything he taught us. I learned a lot from Jimmy Koontz.

He categorized me as a lyric soprano since my voice was light and airy, perfect for music that told a story. To my surprise, he assigned me the solo part for a special number.

My husband would have been proud if he'd been there. He liked hearing me sing and had even slipped into the music room during a rehearsal. He said it reminded him of the day we met, when I was the soloist at a wedding.

Usually, I liked thinking about that day. But during our choir tour, the only memory burning a hole in my brain was the forbidden wine in our refrigerator. I probably should've stayed home even though I wanted to go on the tour. If I had stayed home, I would've dumped the wine by now. It was the simplest solution. We had stashed it because we never threw good things away. But doing so meant keeping secrets, and I was already keeping too many.

If anyone discovered the half-empty bottle in our refrigerator, Denny could lose his job, which would make him look bad. He wasn't bad, but his reputation could be ruined by not following the strict York College standards for students and teachers. And I'd heard that professors who broke the rules might get fired. It was unfair, and I hated it. Thinking like that made me wonder if Denny was as worried as I was.

When the bus stopped for gas, I placed a collect call so I could hear his voice. When the operator asked for my name, I said, "Betty Peal," forgetting I wasn't that girl anymore. Luckily, my hubby recognized my old name.

I said, "Honey, I can't explain how much I miss you. Do you miss me?"

"Betty, I haven't had time."

"I've been gone for five whole hours."

"I know, I know. But right after you left, something happened."

"You got a raise?"

"No. A scandal broke on campus."

"A scandal?"

"Yes. President Bachman wants to fire the football coach."

"Why?"

"For unchristian behavior."

Was he teaching me a lesson or telling me the honest-to-God truth?

Getting Ready to Leave on the York College Choir Bus

He explained. "The coach steals towels from any team that beats us."

"That's all?"

"No, there's more. He cusses with the players."

"And …?"

"Whenever we win, he drinks beer with them."

"Oh, this is *serious*."

My tongue-in-cheek tone flew right over his head, and his next words were heavy with concern. "As the assistant coach, I've seen things that tell me the rumors are true, but I never expected he'd be fired."

"Denny, why are you so upset? Are you and the coach really good buddies?"

"Not at all, but the Ethics Committee will question each faculty member under oath about the accusations. I have to be truthful … and how can I report him when we're hiding wine in our own refrigerator?"

If wine in the refrigerator had been against the law, my dad would've spent most of his life in jail. All I'd wanted to do was learn how to cook with wine. How could that be so wrong?

After Den promised to keep me informed, I shared the situation with his sister and her husband. When Denny's first letter arrived, the three of us huddled close to read the single line: *I transferred the beet juice to a canning jar.*

Glenna said, "I hope he saved the bottle. It had such a pretty grape design molded into the glass."

I said, "Me too. I loved that bottle."

Then a longer letter arrived.

My dearest Betty,

Tomorrow is interrogation day. I flushed the beet juice down the toilet because it had fermented.

Denny

I imagined my dad gasping at the thought of good wine being flushed away.

Denny's impending grilling could flatten our future in a single meeting. He seldom seemed ruffled, so knowing he was upset told me how serious it was. I'd moved way beyond upset. I was so disgusted by all the rigid rules that I wanted to bite someone.

I had experienced the feeling before. The no-dancing rules in my former church were unreasonable, too. The catechism teachings said, "Dancing represents the vertical depiction of a horizontal act." Well, we all knew what they meant by a "horizontal act." Did that mean making a baby was sinful, too? While our church frowned on dancing, members swallowed wine during communion and guzzled beer while playing poker at social events. Other religions permitted congregants to tap their toes and sway while singing in church but considered liquor drinking, card playing, or moviegoing on any day of the week to be sinful activities. Churches created their own rules, and members were expected to hold fast to them.

Enforced obedience, no matter where it happened, caused me to clench my jaw. Denny and I were good people. The thought of him being dismissed because we had wine in our own home disturbed me more than anyone would ever understand. I lingered on those thoughts so long that my stomach was churning as we arrived for our next concert. A churning stomach replaced the music inside of me. On the way to the stage, I whispered to our director, "I think I'm gonna throw up."

"Good grief, Betty! Drop out of line." His piercing whisper caused heads to turn. I couldn't explain to him or to the choir members that I was so angry with the school's rules that I felt sick to my stomach.

With no fanfare, I slipped away to keep from bawling and wandered to the back of the sanctuary, eyes scanning every row for an isolated pew. I had to find a place to relax and reflect on our predicament. Was it possible to stay true to ourselves at York College? Joan of Arc came to mind. What did she think about while being tied to the stake? Did she shriek in protest or quietly give up?

I used an opened hymnal for a pillow, because the inside pages were softer than the cover, and I stretched out flat so no one could see me but God. Then I closed my eyes and listened to the melodious harmonies of our vocalists for the entire concert. Their pure, clear tones distracted me from my worries, and I barely felt the hardness of the bench under my hip bones. An unblocked view of the ceiling hypnotized me, and the music sent thrills down my arms and legs. When the program ended with a tender rendition of "All on an April Evening," tears warmed my cheeks and trickled into my ears. My nose ran like a faucet. I had turned into an emotional mess, caught with no handkerchief, and wiped it all away with the back of my hand. I pleaded silently, *Dear God, Jesus drank wine. Why can't we?*

In the morning, I called Denny. My spirits were lower than earthworms could ever go. When he answered, I said, "Okay, honey, break it to me gently."

He said, "I will. Are you ready?"

"I'm ready."

"Before my turn to be questioned even came up, they had fired the coach."

I almost fainted from relief and couldn't wait to tell Carl and Glenna. I felt guilty that someone else got fired for drinking beer instead of us for harboring wine.

During the long drive to the next location, Dr. Savery offered good news, saying, "You'll be quite pleased to learn that our efforts increased the coming year's enrollment at York College to an all-time high of 318 students." Our recruiter could retire with pride, even though being prideful was a sin.

Applauding and screaming filled the bus, sounding as though we'd won a football game. When visions of the coach drinking, stealing, and cussing sneaked into my thoughts, I swept them out like dirt on a porch.

We performed our last concert in Southern California, where we all got to stretch out on warm sand and swim in the ocean. I had never seen an ocean before, and my body loved the balmy weather and salty air. I wished Denny could've been there, because I longed to see him.

When we got back to York, Denny welcomed us with a simple dinner he'd fixed by himself. It touched me. I noticed he looked kind of gray and faded. I figured he hadn't eaten well during the awful weeks we'd been away.

If Carl and Glenna noticed his washed-out appearance, they kept it to themselves. After giving thanks for our many blessings, Carl said, "Hey, Auch, did you dump all that Mannyshevvy, or did you pour some on these pork chops?"

He said, "Not on your life. That stuff traumatized me, so I dumped all of it."

Glenna said, "I loved that pretty bottle."

"The fancy decanter was a real pain. I wrapped it in five layers of newspaper, wound string around it, and put it in a gunnysack. After the boys went to sleep, I snuck to the basement with a hammer and whacked the daylights out of it. There was nothin' left but loose glass."

"What did you do with that mess?"

"I pushed the bag deep into the garbage can." Denny's shoulders sagged and his face turned solemn. "Glenna, if Mom and Dad found out that I bought wine and started sneaking around, they'd be devastated."

Glenna crossed her arms, acting tough, and said, "They'll get nuttin' outta me."

Carl shoved his thumb in her direction and said, "I'm wid her."

My sweetie seemed unaware of their silly act. I noticed, and it made me laugh. He turned to me and said, "It's not funny."

"I'm sorry, hon." I meant it.

Damn. What had happened to his sense of humor? Or had I failed to notice that he had none? I'd been so lovesick that I married him first and planned to get to know him later.

Later had finally happened.

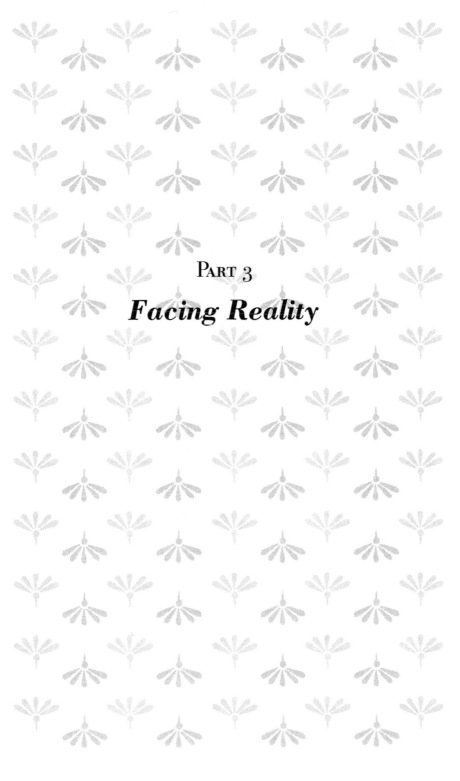

PART 3

Facing Reality

Thompson Hall

CHAPTER 10

The Missing Thing

OUR NEWLYWED PASSION MEANT THAT MY HUSBAND AND I MADE love two or three times a week. One week, we both got so busy that we fell off that schedule. After seven days had passed, I was pretty sure that night would be it. In case he had the same idea, I wanted to be prepared ahead of time. But where was my diaphragm?

I searched every inch of our apartment, but my birth-control device had vanished. I was too embarrassed about misplacing such a personal item to ask Denny for help. We hadn't been married long enough to chat comfortably about the intimate details of birth control. I wasn't sure we'd ever be married long enough for *that* to happen.

Luckily, he stayed up late grading papers, which gave me another day to find it. As soon as he left for classes the next morning, I continued the search, making a muddle of our tidy apartment. Then I heard footsteps on the porch and assumed it was Denny. How would I explain the mess I'd made?

I looked up to see a stooped, white-haired man walking through my front door. He seemed surprised to see me in my own house and said, "I need to use the toilet." He headed straight for the bathroom, and I stood stiff as a pole in the middle of the living room. The old man appeared harmless, but my brain was so addled I couldn't budge. Without moving from the spot, I tried to imagine myself as tall and formidable. I mentally guarded my palace, all the while wondering who the guy was and why he was taking so long. A few minutes later,

I heard the toilet flush. The elderly intruder emerged, shuffled past me, and left through the front door without saying goodbye.

What a creepy experience. I didn't know whether to report it or just forget about the incident. When Denny came home for lunch, I would tell him about the mystery man, and he could help me decide. I resumed the search for my missing item, but my mind kept drifting to the stranger who had crossed our threshold as if he owned the place.

When I told my husband about our uninvited guest, he said, "Describe him."

"He had a bent back and white hair, and he wore a brown cardigan."

My husband brushed the air with his hand, as he often did, and said, "Oh, him. Don't worry, Betty. That's old Dr. Feemster."

"You *know* him?"

"Sure. He's one of the few people who truly understands Einstein's theory of relativity. He taught advanced scientific concepts, his daughter is a brilliant anthropologist, and—"

I butted in. "And now he breaks into homes to go potty?"

If eyebrows could talk, Denny's had just said, "Excuse me?" My smart-aleck remark had surprised him as much as it surprised me. I felt ashamed. Then his eyes softened, which meant he was getting back to the subject. He said, "Dr. Feemster must've been lost. Some of his memories are lost, too. He's alone now and loves taking walks near the campus. He knows everyone in this neighborhood, and most of them understand why he drops in uninvited."

"This has happened before?"

"Oh, sure, lots of times."

"I'm lockin' the front door right now."

He frowned and said, "Betty, people in York, Nebraska, don't lock their doors during the day."

"So let me be the first."

"Dr. Feemster is forgetful, but he's harmless. He'll be even more confused if he can't get in to use our bathroom. We all accommodate him."

I agreed to leave our front door unlocked, but the thought of another visit unnerved me. Then Denny looked down at his feet instead of meeting my eyes and said, "Uh, while we're on the subject … you forgot to flush again."

I felt my face burn with embarrassment. Why was it so hard to remember that? Most of the houses my family rented had an outhouse, so I'd never gotten used to indoor toilets. My spouse didn't consider that a good excuse.

He returned to his afternoon classes after lunch, leaving me in a mess of emotions. I felt ashamed about losing such a personal item and ill at ease about a stranger borrowing my bathroom. I was embarrassed, anxious, and a little angry that Denny had reminded me to flush. I kept forgetting my new last name and often identified myself as Betty Peal on the telephone. I wasn't getting anything right.

I tried to shake off the emotional overload and get back to the business at hand. *Let's see … what was I doing before the old man walked into my house? Oh, yes, looking for my diaphragm.*

Then the possibility popped into my head that the boys had hidden my gizmo. They'd pulled pranks before and had probably stuck it in the same place they stashed our bedroom key before I was carried over the threshold five months earlier. I hurried to the refrigerator to scan the tiny ice cube tray. Nothing there but frost-covered ice cubes, which reminded me that I needed to ask Glenna how to defrost the freezer.

Living in Thompson Hall with religious boys on the second floor had become a devilish partnership. I wanted to pound up the stairs, plant myself in the hall with arms folded across my chest like John Wayne, and bellow, "Okay, you guys, which one of you stole my private property?" That's when Denny, the role model, would likely make another untimely entrance and remind me of my duties as a faculty wife. I cancelled that dumb idea … too confrontational.

Besides, it would be really embarrassing it they had nothing to do with it. Glenna and Carl, on the other hand— Playful theft was certainly something they might do. They were in our apartment a lot and could be the culprits. I dialed their number, twisted a lock of hair into a tangled mess, and waited. Finally, my sister-in-law answered with a polite greeting.

"Hello, this is Glenna Bott."

"Did you guys hide my diaphragm?"

"Betty, is that you?"

"Yes, it is. Did you guys steal it?"

"What?" Glenna exploded in laughter. She struggled to reply. "You lost your diaphragm? Maybe you're still wearing it."

I hadn't thought of that. I got off the phone fast and rushed to the bathroom to check it out. Sure as shootin', there it was, tucked around my cervix where it had been for the last seven days. That couldn't be good; it might even be dangerous.

I called the doctor for advice. He said simply, "Take it out."

"Doctor, I did. But shouldn't I be examined to see if there's any damage?"

"What kind of damage?"

"Um, like an infection or something?"

"No, you'll be fine. Don't worry about it." He laughed, so I laughed, though I didn't think it was funny. I felt like an idiot. So many unexpected events had popped up in my new life that not worrying would take a miracle. Instead, I just added four new items to my growing list, which I titled *Important Stuff to Remember:*

· Keep doors locked no matter what Denny says.

· Flush every time.

· Find out how to defrost the freezer.

· Remove diaphragm when not in use.

Being a wife was way more work than I'd ever imagined.

CHAPTER II

Surrogate Sister

I WAS THE SAME AGE AS THE BOYS IN THOMPSON HALL, SO I NEVER felt like their surrogate mother. It seemed more like I was a surrogate sister living with twelve brothers. Not all kids in large families get along, and I was no exception. I took an immediate dislike to one guy in the house. I felt so ill at ease around him that I didn't even like his girlfriend, which was pretty dumb of me. I couldn't understand why I felt so strongly about Dick.

It might've been because he never looked directly at my face when we talked. Instead, he studied my ear or shoulder. He often kept his eyes lowered, which made him look guilty of something. I thought maybe he was self-conscious about his large nose and receding chin. He seemed so uncomfortable around people that I couldn't imagine why he'd majored in theology. If he graduated, Dick might be a very sinister minister ... unless his fine tenor singing voice managed to save the day.

Dick's girlfriend, Abby, agreed with everyone. When she took part in conversations, she always reiterated what she heard, contributing no original thoughts, like riding a bus without paying the fare. A few gossipy girls referred to her privately as "Little Miss Echo," because she reminded them of *Little Sir Echo,* the hit song Bing Crosby had made famous.

Abby had naturally curly hair, a gorgeous complexion, and a pleasingly plump body with no corners anywhere. Her rosy cheeks were so chubby it appeared she hoarded acorns inside of them.

79

Dick and Abby were hot to trot, and the parlor was their favorite place to neck. Their carnal obsession with each other interfered with my cleaning schedule. When I explained this to Denny, he said, "Just tell them to come back after you vacuum the rug."

"Are you kidding? I'd be too embarrassed to ask them to leave."

So I accommodated the annoying couple rather than interrupting and checked the room again in fifteen minutes. By that time their passion had usually worn off, and they were gone.

The other boy who made me mad enough to chew nails went hunting one day and came home carrying a gunnysack. He opened it to show me six small game hens shot dead.

"Oh, Henry, they were just babies."

"Nope. Guinea hens are always real little. Would you cook 'em for me?"

"Sure, if you do all the icky stuff first."

He needed clarification. "By icky stuff, do you mean removing the feathers and guts?"

"Yep, that's what I mean."

The project intrigued me. I could use two of my wedding presents: the blue enamel roasting pan and my *Better Homes and Gardens* cookbook.

He returned with the birds cleaned and ready for the roaster. In an hour, their skin looked shiny and crisp. The aroma was so tantalizing I picked off a piece of meat in a place that didn't show. It tasted delicious. I hoped he would say, "Since I've got six of these, keep two for you and Auch." When he didn't offer, I wished I'd ripped off a whole leg and left a gaping hole.

Henry rushed off with his succulent birds and my roaster, saying, "I'll bring the pan back later." I heard the boys upstairs giving him a bad time for eating all six hens in front of them. His thoughtlessness irked me, but I had to forget about it and fix *our* supper. My husband never tired of tuna noodle casserole.

After dinner, Henry knocked on our door and returned my roasting pan, empty but unwashed. If I'd been more mature and experienced, I would have grounded him for sure.

The next day I cleaned the house while the boys were in class. I toted my bag of rags and cleansers to their bathroom and opened the door, ready to whistle while I worked. The sight that greeted me instantly squelched any tunes I had in mind. Feathers were everywhere, and disgusting stuff filled the sink and wastebasket. I was appalled that Henry the Hunter had cleaned his birds in the bathroom instead of outside. While thinking how much I'd like to roast his hide 'til *he* turned crispy, I forced myself to clean up the mess.

Why I said nothing to him was a mystery to me, and I was terribly annoyed with myself for avoiding the confrontation. I could light out after someone who shot me with a water pistol, but I froze when one of the boys deserved a bawling out. Maybe I could blame my parents. They had verbal confrontations all the time about trivial matters. I did the opposite by smilin' through and keepin' the peace. Once more, I promised myself to be less generous in the future, but it was hard, because I was addicted to pleasing everyone.

I didn't tell Denny about the episode for two reasons. I was afraid he might've said, "Betty, don't worry about it," which would've added to my irritation. I also dreaded the possibility that he might bawl Henry out, and I didn't want the guy mad at me, even though he was near the bottom of my "like" list. As an active member of the Gutless Girls Club, I rarely stood up for myself.

That night after dinner, Denny asked, "Are you in the mood for root beer floats?"

A frosty root beer over ice cream was just what I needed to lift my mood from the doldrums. "Heck, yes," I replied. "I'm in the mood."

While Denny headed to the store for the ingredients, I began cleaning up the dishes. I'd barely started washing them when he returned. Without looking up from the dishpan, I said, "Forgot the car keys, didn't you?"

"No … Dick and Abby are making out in our back seat."

Suddenly, we were both whispering. "You've *got* to be kidding."

"No, I'm not kidding."

"Were you embarrassed?"

"Oh, yeah."

"What did you say?"

"I said, 'Oh, sorry,' and closed the door." Denny could start a cowardly club, too.

"Honey, how long do you think they'll take?"

"I don't know. Maybe I should go ask 'em."

I knew he was kidding.

Half an hour later, he took a chance and crept out to our car. After reporting that Dick and Abby had left, he drove to the store to pick up the makings for our favorite dessert.

That night I added three more items to my *Important Stuff to Remember* list:

· Put a sign in the boys' bathroom that says *No blood, feathers, or guts allowed.*

· Post a sign that says *No necking in our car or the parlor.*

· Take deep breaths and stay calm.

Being a housemother was no easier than being a wife.

Lovers in Our Car

CHAPTER 12

Life Happens

IN MAY OF 1950, WE'D BEEN MARRIED SIX MONTHS WHEN DENNY commented on our apartment. He said, "Betty, don't you think our living room is kinda boring?"

"Yeah, it's boring. And ugly."

"What can we do about it?"

"I think we should paint the walls."

"That would be easy, and we could do it in a day. But we can't change a thing without permission from the college treasurer."

"Then get permission! They'll probably pay for the paint if we do the work." I wanted to start that minute.

The college treasurer was a friend with whom we'd spent many evenings playing Yahtzee in our living room. After allowing her to win one night, we mentioned our plan. Denny said, "Helen Jo, you've probably noticed the dowdy appearance of our apartment."

"Well, yes, I have, but used furnishings are what the college can afford."

"If Betty and I do the work, can the college pay for some paint?"

Her raised eyebrows said, "Not a chance in hell." Her voice said, "Denny, we can't afford any upgrades, but you can spiff things up if you cover the expenses."

What a letdown. We could barely make ends meet, but after mulling it over, I said, "Let's just do it." And we did.

Painting was not as simple as we'd assumed, because countless layers of wallpaper had to be removed first. We spread drop cloths to protect the floor and rented a steamer that looked like a vacuum cleaner. Then Denny and I softened and peeled off piles of yuck. It became so labor intensive that I forgot my painting urges and attacked the slimy mess as though I hated the walls. What a dirty job. It took several days, but we finally scraped our way right down to the plaster. I was then surrounded by blank white surfaces waiting for my artistic statement. I convinced my hubby that chartreuse walls would liven up the room.

The yellow-green color jazzed it up so much that, by comparison, the down-and-out furniture resembled archeological finds. We didn't have the means to replace anything, but we could rent a machine to shampoo the rug and then camouflage the couch and chair with accessories. It meant spending more money, but what the heck.

We went shopping for colorful throw pillows at Sears and Roebuck. While there, I noticed plastic floor-length drapes on sale for $3.49 a panel. Four panels were all we needed for our naked windows. The design featured king-sized blossoms with smidgens of bright green, which went well with the walls. The purchases brought our dead living room back to life.

Even though steaming, scraping, and painting had worn us out, the end result filled me with joy. If rooms could talk, mine would have proclaimed, "This is where Betty lives!" I had never before had an opportunity to make such a bold personal statement. What made it even better was that Denny liked the result as much as I did.

To my surprise, Carl, Glenna, and Helen Jo considered our color choices garish. While other people might have preferred playing it safe with muted hues, such as variations of tan, Denny and I were delighted with our lively décor. I floated on the feeling of being in control of something for a change.

While still riding my living room high, we invited Carl and Glenna to our apartment for one of our traditional leftover dinners. By combining whatever lurked in our refrigerators, Glenna and I created a good-enough meal for all four of us. Next on our list of favorite things to do was a stroll to the store for ice cream. But a crudely printed sign stopped all forward movement. It read: *Six-week-old terriers for sale.* What fun to watch them climbing all over each other in their pen while chewing each other's tails and yapping little puppy messages. I heard, "Arf, arf. Pick me, pick me." Oh, the memories that flooded my thoughts. My family had never been without a dog. I wasn't the only person in our group who wanted a furry pet. We all did. Instead of returning home with ice cream, we arrived with puppies.

Carl and Glenna picked a black-and-white female, and Denny and I chose her tan-and-white sister. We named ours Chipper, but they couldn't agree on a name and temporarily called theirs Doggie. Chipper and Doggie were siblings who never fought. They were so compatible we decided to leave them together in our apartment for the weekend while visiting my in-laws in Kansas.

Our pups had access to the kitchen and living room. We covered the freshly cleaned living room rug with newspapers and left them two bowls of water, two bowls of kibbles, two doggie blankets, and a few toys. They could eat, drink, poop, and pee on the paper and sleep on their own little blankets. As the last one out, Denny turned the lamp on low, and we left, knowing that our pets' needs were covered.

Leaving two pups alone for two days had been insane, but we were young and didn't know as much as we thought we knew. Upon arriving home, I noticed from the street that our plastic drapes looked shorter. Once inside, we took turns gasping out a few words.

Glenna: "Oh, no."

Carl: "What in the world?"

Denny: "I can't believe this."

Me: "What were we thinking?"

Our adorable little pets had spilled their water, knocked over the food bowls, chewed the newspapers into shreds, and apparently took turns seeing which puppy could jump the highest and take the biggest bite out of the drapes. Brightly colored hunks of plastic blended with puppy poops and pee, resembling an unusual art form. Both dogs were over the moon with wiggles and happiness to see us, but we couldn't even pet them. They looked and smelled like they'd had a great time rolling around in their art project.

That mess led to several days of cleaning. We threw the drapes away, shampooed the carpet again, and purged our apartment of the stench. We were truly tuckered out by the time Denny said, "We've gotta put our puppy problems behind us and get ready for the Y Club picnic and wiener roast."

My husband was the club sponsor, so it wasn't an event we could miss. We put our doggie on a leash and took her with us. Chipper got passed around because she was so cute that everyone wanted a turn. While she was the center of attention, it gave me a chance to notice how much respect and admiration the football team had for my husband.

Hot dogs and potato chips were the typical fare, followed by bonfire-blackened marshmallows squished between chunks of Hershey Bar and graham crackers. Dessert was pure sugar joy.

After dessert, the guys got busy creating a small make-do baseball diamond, and all of us girls sat around the grassy edges cheering for our men. As annual events go, that crude baseball game was as important to the boys as season playoffs. Spots of dirt and bumps in grass evolved into home plate, first base, and second base. A huge log passed for third base. If any player made a rare home run, he could breeze right past the log without running into it. But my guy barely made it to third base, where he slammed into the log so hard that I sucked in my breath. He picked himself up and waited for an opportunity to score another point.

Then Chuck, the Thompson Hall fellow with whom I'd had a water pistol shootout, tripped, launched himself *over* the log, and landed on the ground, writhing in pain. It was a frightening thing to watch. I thought he'd broken his leg, but one of the players said, "It's not broken. This happens to Chuck all the time in football practice; his knee has gone out."

I didn't know what a knee going out meant, but it must've been bad, because the ball game came to a halt. What a sad way to end a happy day.

I worried about our boy, Chuck. By the next morning he was in good shape, which reassured me. But Denny woke up exhausted and said, "Gosh, I hurt all over."

"Too much softball?"

"Probably, because I had a knee ache last night and couldn't get comfortable."

He brushed it off because we had plans to leave the next morning for a six-hour drive to the state teacher's college in Greeley, Colorado. We had to find a rental for summer school so he could finish his master's degree in mathematics.

I asked, "Shouldn't you see the doctor before we leave?"

"I don't need a doctor. I'll be fine."

I wasn't so sure. His limping and taking aspirin told me he wasn't fine at all.

Betty, Chipper, and the Car

CHAPTER 13

The Terrible Trip

IN THE MIDDLE OF THE SCHOOL YEAR, OUR FRIENDS BOB AND WILMA Gillespie joined the physical education department at York College. It was at their wedding that Denny and I first met. Bob had graduated from York, but Wilma was new to campus. I considered it my duty to warn her of the strict guidelines for conduct. She brushed off my concern with a breezy "I'll be fine." I knew she wouldn't be fine, and she soon found that out for herself.

Wilma taught tennis and folk dancing. When she learned that the college prohibited dancing of any kind, she wanted to quit before she'd even started. We didn't want them to leave, so we talked her into changing the name of her class. The four of us came up with a new title, which she presented to the administrative board. They said, "That works for us." The board members were thrilled when Wilma's *Folk Games* class filled to overflowing, and we patted ourselves on the back for being so clever.

Late in May, before the end of the school year, Wilma, Bob, Denny, and I drove to Greeley, Colorado, to find housing for summer school. Carl and Glenna took care of Chipper so she could play with her sister, Doggie. With no time to waste, we searched the ads for cheap apartments. Because Denny earned very little money at York College, we couldn't be choosy. For six weeks, we needed only a place to eat, sleep, shower, and finish a master's thesis.

Near the end of the first day, we found a one-room rental in a garage that might work. It reminded me of the one-room shed my family had lived in seven years earlier. We parked our 1947 two-door Dodge coupe in the alley and rang the back doorbell. Although the garage apartment was barely tolerable, the landlords seemed pleasant. We could've looked for something nicer, but by that point we didn't give a hoot. Denny's pain and fatigue were getting worse, and I was getting worried. I wanted to sign a lease and go home.

While we prepared to drive away, another vehicle zoomed down the alley and came to a screeching halt next to us. The angry-looking driver rolled down his window. I recognized the man, though he would not have known me. Dr. and Mrs. Hollenberg had been houseparents in Gordon Hall during my freshman year. I'd seen them every night in the dining room and remembered her gracious nature and his abrasive personality. His degrading comments didn't surprise me at all.

He said, "Sir, can't you read?"

"Read?"

"The sign that says 'No parking'?"

Denny glanced around for a sign. "I'm sorry. We were just looking at this apartment for summer school."

"Well, you'd better not park *here* this summer." With that, he sped away.

What an awful welcome. We felt stunned and insulted.

Shaking off the encounter, we drove to the front of the house to see where we *might* park when the time came. Cars lined the street. Resigned that parking would be a problem, I said, "I guess we'll have to find someplace nearby to leave the car and not drive it. Walking to campus will be good for you." I hoped I was right.

I forced myself to be positive while riding to our cheap hotel, but my husband seemed unnaturally quiet. Maybe the rude professor was still on his mind. I asked, "Hon, are you upset?"

"No. I'm not upset. It's just that my knee really hurts."

"Den, after we get back to York, you've gotta make an appointment."

"I will. I will. But my knee is killing me now, and I need something stronger than aspirin."

Our hotel was downtown, close to Adams Pharmacy, so we asked the druggist what we could purchase. He said, "Don't take anything new until you talk to your doctor." In desperation, Den bought a pack of cigarettes and a book of matches. I asked why.

"One of the guys in the house told me that smoking a cigarette can take your mind off pain. At this point, I'll try anything."

Once in the hotel room, he headed for the bathroom, saying, "I'm gonna light up in here, but I don't want Bob and Wilma sniffing smoke. I'll turn on the exhaust fan."

I had been a willing partner in deceit when we hid the wine and now readily participated in the cigarette caper. We sat on the edge of the tub while he tried to figure out how to open the package.

I said, "You pull this little red tag."

"How could you know that?" he asked.

I reminded him that my parents kept the tobacco industry busy. My little brother had attempted to follow their example when he was nine by lighting up a twig in our cornstalk teepee. He wanted to learn how to smoke and almost burned us alive instead. In a panic, Dad rescued us and explained that dried cornstalks were even more flammable than twigs. A few years later, I tried to smoke a dried, hollow stick, and it burst into flames. You'd think I would've learned a lesson from my brother's experience. Apparently, I was dumber than Bobby. But this time I wasn't the person doing the smoking. I just wanted to help ease Denny's discomfort.

My ailing husband sat on the edge of the tub while I perched on the closed toilet seat. He looked awkward and uncomfortable as he lit up while barely holding the cigarette between his thumb and forefinger, as if he expected it to poison him. I don't think he knew how to inhale, because he kept blowing smoke out of his mouth real fast. All I could do was watch, wanting to help and feeling useless. He finally gave up and said, "To heck with this." It was too hard learning how to smoke under pressure, and we knew our friends might knock on the door any minute. After flushing the thing down the toilet, he tossed the package into the waste can and turned the exhaust fan to high. The tiny room reeked of tobacco smoke, so he opened the windows.

When our friends did knock, he became frantic and swooshed air toward the nearest window with both hands. Keeping his voice low, he said, "Betty, help me push this outta here." Then he called out to Bob and Wilma. "We're dressing. Meet us downstairs in the coffee shop." We pushed and fanned the air double time, hoping they hadn't gotten a whiff.

Over hamburgers, Bob and Wilma announced that they, too, had found a place to rent and suggested we check out of the hotel and drive back to Nebraska after dinner. It would be a relief to get home.

⚜

THAT NIGHT DENNY SUFFERED THROUGH A FITFUL SLEEP, CHANGING his position constantly in an effort to get comfortable. My concern intensified, but I stayed as calm as possible. The next morning, he called Dr. James Bell to explain how he had slammed into the third-base tree trunk while playing baseball at the picnic and that his leg had bothered him ever since. He said, "My knee is the real problem, but my whole body hurts."

The doctor said, "This doesn't sound good. You need to come in immediately for some tests."

"Tests?"

"Yes, let's see what's going on. We'll do lab tests first and then take x-rays."

We left for the doctor's office as soon as Denny hung up the phone. After the procedures, we sat as still as mannequins for an hour, both of us immersed in our own private thoughts. Mine bounced between hope and fear.

Finally, Dr. Bell called us in to view the x-rays. I didn't know what the inside of bones should look like, but the doctor gestured in circles with a little wand, describing what we were seeing. "This is a tumor inside the marrow of your tibia. It's at the top of that bone, near the knee joint. As you can see, it's filling up the whole cavity. This thin line of bone surrounding the tumor should be thicker."

I stopped breathing for a moment at the word *tumor*, while Denny asked, "How much thicker?"

"Well, let me put it this way. It should be like a wall, but yours is more like a shell."

"A shell?"

"Yes. It's thin enough to break if you even bump your knee."

"So ... what do we do next?"

"We schedule surgery as soon as possible so we can take a biopsy."

Dr. Bell's composure did not rub off on us. Denny swallowed and said, "Biopsy?"

"Yes. Let's hope it's not malignant."

"Malignant?"

His one-word questions unnerved me.

Dr. Bell looked at his shoes for a second and said, "You may as well know up front ... if it's malignant, it means above-the-knee amputation."

I held my breath again, not knowing what to say. This time Denny was quiet, too. We were struck silent in disbelief. The nurse brought crutches for him to use while waiting for surgery, and I was so lost in thought that I stared at them like I'd never seen crutches before. None of it seemed real. The words *malignant* and *amputation* sounded serious but were so foreign to my vocabulary that I refused to let them take root inside my head. Instead, I imagined possible scenarios. If he lost part of his leg, they'd replace it with a prosthetic. If the cancer spread, they would treat it. If it wasn't cancer, his wound would heal, and we'd get on with our lives. I refused to believe he might die. He was too young.

On our way out, Dr. Bell stopped us, put his hand on my husband's shoulder, and said, "Don't forget that the bone around the tumor is thin as a shell. If you fall down, you'll break your knee."

Denny just nodded and said nothing.

I said, "I'll make sure that doesn't happen, Doctor." I had no idea how I'd keep my husband safe, but I was determined to try.

CHAPTER 14

A Gory Story

THE SERIOUS NATURE OF DENNY'S KNEE INJURY BROUGHT HIS parents from Kansas to Nebraska. I had planned to be with my in-laws at the hospital before, during, and after the operation. At the last minute, I backed out because my monthly cramps were worse than usual.

I stayed home in bed with Midol® and a hot water bottle, thankful for a legitimate reason to be absent during the surgery. Why? Because my attempts at positive thinking had been masking unadulterated fear about the whole scary ordeal. I was terrified that something horrible might happen, and I wanted it to be over.

When my father-in-law filled me in later on what took place in the operating room, I was relieved that I hadn't been there. The doctor had told my husband's parents that they could watch the surgery through a window. His father accepted the offer, but his mother chose to sit in the waiting lounge, where she could read the Bible and pray. The operation so fascinated Denny's father that he described it to me in more detail than I could handle.

Apparently, the mass in my husband's knee had grown so fast that it caused extreme pressure. When they drilled through the bone and pierced the tumor, it literally exploded, splattering the ceiling of the operating room. Reverend Auchard said the doctors were so surprised that they jumped away from the table, and one dropped his scalpel. My father-in-law had a reputation for stretching the truth, but this was not one of those times, because Den told me it really happened.

He'd been awake during the surgery but numb from the waist down. He heard the sound of the drill going through the bone and saw the eruption that startled the surgical team.

DR. BELL SENT A SAMPLE OF THE TUMOR TO THE LAB IN OMAHA AND explained that we'd know the results in a week. If the biopsy turned out positive, they'd wheel Denny back into surgery for above-the-knee amputation.

As soon as they knew their son had survived the surgery, Den's parents returned home so Reverend Auchard could prepare Sunday's sermon. I had faked courage so they wouldn't witness how truly scared I was. I didn't want to give them more to worry about, and I didn't want to appear frail and helpless. I'd planned to sob my fear away once they left, but my plans didn't work out. Soon after the Auchards headed for Kansas, my fifteen-year-old sister, Patty, showed up at the door, all the way from Denver. Crying would have to wait a little longer, but down deep, I was glad to see her.

"Patty, what a surprise. How did you get here?"

"By bus. Mom didn't want you to be alone, but she said not to be talkin' about Denny's leg. I'm supposed to lift your spirits and help get your mind on something else."

"Well, Patty, you know what'll happen if we don't mind Mom."

"We'll get a lickin'. So, what shall we do first? We could go for a walk on the campus."

I already felt better, but I had another destination in mind. "Let's go visit the patient. I'll drive."

"I thought you didn't know how to drive."

"I do now. I got my license. Driving back and forth to see my sweetie every day will be good practice."

That was true, but what I really wanted to do was hold his hand and tell him everything would be fine. Denial was so much easier than facing reality.

I had never been to the hospital. The antiseptic odor, hushed tones, and glossy floors created an eerie atmosphere that added to my nervousness. After my sister and I made our way to Denny's room, we found him in a deep, sedated sleep. Patty stiffened and asked, "Is he dead?"

"No, Patty, he's alive. That's the way he looks when he's asleep." Denial again. He actually looked like he was near death's door.

The nurse said he wouldn't be awake until noon, so we left, but my husband's lifeless image went with me. For Patty's sake, I'd been casual about how awful he looked, but I could think of nothing else, not even my driving. While backing out of the parking space, I almost sideswiped a parked Cadillac. Patty yelled "Stop!" just in time, but the near miss scared me silly.

Clutching her chest to keep her heart in place, my sister said, "Betty, please, let's hitchhike or call a cab tomorrow. I'm afraid to ride with you." I was still so nervous that I laughed hysterically. So did my sister, and our jaws soon hurt from laughing. Patty's presence *did* lift my spirits, and with each trip, my driving improved.

After Patty returned to Colorado, I practiced cruising all over town between trips to Denny's room. I enjoyed it immensely, which had an oddly positive effect on me. Behind the wheel, I transformed into a responsible, capable adult, even though I didn't know how to put gas in the car. I covered up that flaw by paying close attention to the arrow displaying the amount left in the tank. I figured someone could teach me how to fill it up before the pointer reached empty.

DURING MY NEXT VISIT TO THE HOSPITAL, I TOOK A DETOUR TO another ward, where our friend Opal lay recuperating from a burst appendix. Instead of greeting me, she said with some urgency, "Oh, my goodness. Have you talked to Denny today?"

"Not yet. I wanted to find out how you were doing first."

"This morning he screamed. You'd better check on him."

"He screamed?"

"Twice."

"*Twice?*"

"Yeah, really loud. You could hear him all over the place."

I ran to his room with a sense of panic surging through my body. Before I got inside the door, a nurse stopped me and said, "Your husband is pretty shaky today." I was pretty shaky myself and asked, "What happened?"

"We changed the dressing, and it's an uncomfortable procedure." The nurse explained that a three-inch square had been cut out of the cast, which opened like a lid. "That's how we change the gauze dressing inside the bone."

I tried not to picture it, but my imagination wouldn't let it go.

Denny looked pale and exhausted. I asked, "How're you doin', hon?"

"Betty, I had a terrible experience this morning. The nurse pulled a long piece of bloody gauze out of my knee. I hadn't expected unbearable pain."

"Oh, honey."

"Then I heard a scream and realized it came from me. When it was over, I went limp." I laid my hand on his arm to comfort him while he talked. "Then she reached inside the cast with big tweezers and pulled out another long piece, and a scream came out of me again."

I clasped my hand to my mouth, knowing there was still more to his story.

He continued. "I thought it was over, but it wasn't. She squirted medicine in the hole and pushed in new gauze. That's when I passed out."

Hearing that he'd passed out from the pain made the possibility of his leg being cut off seem real, and a black cloud settled over my shoulders. If the biopsy proved to be malignant, what kind of future could we possibly have? I barely hid my fear.

WAITING FOR THE WEEK TO PASS WAS TORTURE. I VACILLATED BETWEEN positive thinking and active denial. I wasn't there when Dr. Bell poked his head into my husband's room and said, "Good news: no malignancy."

Den told me about it a few hours later, saying, "I burst into sobs and couldn't stop."

He wept again, with palms pressed to his eyes as though holding them in his head. Witnessing his state of mind made me realize how frightened he'd been and how close we'd come to the real thing. I had taken a vacation from the truth, but he hadn't. Tears blurred my vision. I shut his door, and we cried ourselves dry.

Before the hospital released Den, a nurse changed the gauze pack again. The tissue had healed a bit, which made it easier. At home, Carl and Glenna propped him up in the upholstered chair, elevated his feet, brought extra food, hugged us, and left. Then he became *my* patient. He was practically an invalid. Exhaling a noisy sigh, he said, "Betty, I feel helpless, but I'm not complaining. Look! I have two legs and two wooden crutches."

I felt positive again.

Denny looked forward to the prospect of a walking cast. It would provide mobility and help him get stronger. While we waited for that time to come, my mother decided to visit and help out. A tad bit of dread spoiled my happy frame of mind, because hosting Mom was quite a different experience from hosting my sister. Patty and I were like girlfriends. Mom would try to fix anything she felt hadn't been done right. But I felt I should stop expecting the worse and be grateful for her help.

My mother cooked and cleaned, and I truly appreciated her efforts. Then one day, out of nowhere, she said, "Betty, your boobs look bigger. Are you pregnant?"

"No, Mom, I'm not pregnant."

"You know, doncha, that once a woman starts having sex, her boobs grow."

That kind of information, especially coming from my mother, embarrassed me. Later, she mentioned that the wedding dress we had worked so hard to make should have been dry-cleaned and packed away. I honestly didn't know that. She told me that the sweat stains would eventually turn yellow. My newfound sense of being an adult was fading fast.

My mother's never-ending advice didn't bother my husband, but it drove me crazy. She started sniffing the air, saying, "Somewhere in this apartment, a dead mouse is rotting."

I said, "Mom, you're smelling Denny's bandages, not a dead mouse."

She cleaned the whole apartment anyway, hoping to find that rotting rodent. I made a sincere effort to continue feeling thankful she was there, while wondering how soon she might leave.

A week later, I took my patient back to the doctor's office so they could replace the stinky dressings and clean up his leg. They removed the old cast and gave him one he could walk in. He hobbled and clunked around our apartment so my mother would notice his non-invalid status. Once he'd convinced Mom we could manage on our own, she returned to Denver. My body and mind finally relaxed.

❦

DENNY CANCELED EVERYTHING WE'D ARRANGED IN GREELEY, Colorado, including his summer school classes and our rented garage apartment. He would have to stay in York and work on his master's project while his leg healed. Our prospective landlords, who had seemed so gracious, turned rude when they learned we had to cancel. My anger rose up, but Den waved his hand like he always did and said, "Betty, don't worry about it." He was becoming his old self again.

Because he couldn't drive, he became my passenger, and it made me uptight. He flinched whenever I ground the gears, which meant he was even more nervous than I. We agreed that a car with an automatic shift would be less stressful for both of us while he was my passenger and would eventually enable him to operate the pedals using only his good leg. The next day, we traded our Dodge coupe for a 1950 Pontiac. I was so excited that I would have driven every day if we'd had someplace to go.

❋

AFTER THE CAST CAME OFF FOR GOOD, A BANDAGE PROTECTED THE wound while new bone grew over the hole. Joy infused my being, and I felt glad to be alive. Eventually, we put the cancer scare behind us.

All that remained was a caved-in spot in the middle of Denny's right knee below the kneecap. Bone never grew enough to fill the indentation. Forty years later, our young grandson often said, "Papa, show me that hole in your knee again." He would examine it closely before saying, "I wanna hear the story again ... the one about how they almost cut off your leg."

"Papa" repeated the entire story over and over, including the exploding tumor that hit the ceiling and the screaming and crying scenes. The grandkids never got tired of hearing the details, because kids seem to love gory stories.

Me? I'm glad it's history.

❋

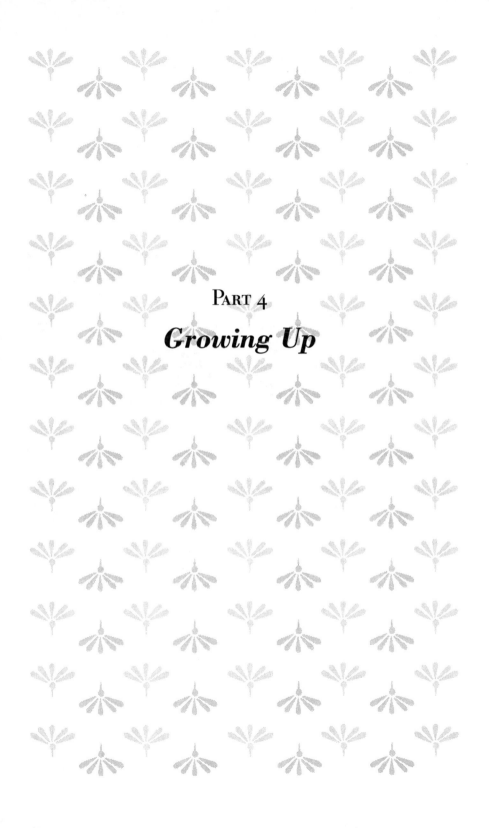

PART 4
Growing Up

The York College Administration Building (Old Main) Burns

Chapter 15

Flames and Ashes

ON JANUARY 3, 1951, THE LOW TEMPERATURE OUTDOORS KEPT everyone indoors. I wanted to stay home myself but couldn't miss weekly choir practice. I hooked a ride with Jimmy Koontz, our director, and he drove me home after the rehearsal. When I started to thank him, he looked over my shoulder and said, "Oh, my God!"

"What?"

"The Ad Building ... I see smoke!"

I looked across the street and gasped, shoved the car door open, and ran to the house, taking the porch steps two at a time. Jimmy called out, "Tell Denny!" and he sped away. I slammed the front door open and yelled, "Smoke is coming out of the Ad Building. Call the fire department!"

Although he appeared calm, Denny's hands trembled as he dialed. When we heard sirens in the distance, he hung up. Someone else had already made the call. Grabbing a jacket, he said, "I've gotta get over there." I followed him outside and saw that people were coming from all directions and heading toward the fire.

When the whine of sirens got closer and louder, our twelve boys poured out of the house and tore across the campus to join the volunteers. Carl and Glenna burst from their apartment across the street, and Carl called out, "What's happening?"

I shouted back. "Old Main's on fire! That's where everyone's headed."

Carl tore off to assist wherever he could, while Glenna and I crossed the street and stayed on the sidelines. Almost to herself, she said, "Oh, my God, I can't believe this." We watched as a group of people carried filing cabinets to safety while another team rescued books from the library next door. It was such a nightmarish scene that I found it impossible to form lucid thoughts. We stood and stared, feeling helpless.

When embers drifted onto the library roof, screams erupted from the crowd, but firemen rushed to squelch the sparks before they could do any damage. I grabbed my sister-in-law's arm to get her attention. "Glenna, where did the guys go?"

She pointed and said, "Carl has been carrying books out and going back for more."

"Could you tell if Denny was with him?"

"I think he's still in the Ad Building."

That was not the reply I'd hoped for. I knew she was probably right, but I'd been praying that Den had left to help out somewhere less dangerous. My heart started hammering when Glenna confirmed my fear that he was in the worst place possible.

We watched in stunned silence as an endless trail of strangers carried cabinets outside and dumped them on the ground. The library group ran as fast as they could with armloads of books hindering their speed. They dropped them wherever they found an empty spot.

More fire engines rumbled onto the campus, blasting horns so people would get out of the way. The power of the flames had accelerated. Smoke leaked from Old Main's second-story windows, and flames crawled along telephone wires. Embers drifted around us, and firefighters bellowed through megaphones, "Clear the building; clear the building." Two volunteers struggled with a cabinet and leaned it against a tree. No one else came after them.

Onlookers yelled, "There are people still inside!" Panic crashed through my body, and my hands slammed against my mouth to keep a scream from escaping. My husband could be trapped in that inferno.

I grabbed Glenna's arm again, this time for moral support. For a few minutes, I floated in limbo, numb and frozen with fear and trying not to imagine what might be happening in the flames. Then I concentrated on Den coming through the ordeal safely.

Finally, someone said, "People are coming out!" My grip on Glenna tightened when I saw Denny running to join us. As soon as he reached our spot, I snatched him close and couldn't let go.

I said, "I thought I'd lost you."

"We barely beat the flames."

"Why were you inside so long?"

"We had to rescue science equipment from the basement labs."

"What kind of equipment could be *that* precious?" My voice sounded strange to my ears, as if it was echoing inside a barrel.

"Anything we could grab ... microscopes and thermometers and even the fan off my desk."

I was horrified that he had risked his life to save a few microscopes and an old fan. I started bawling, and he held me so tight I could feel his heart pounding. We stayed that way 'til I could pull myself together.

I was convinced that picturing him safe had kept him that way. I might be a married woman and a houseparent to twelve college-age boys, but I still believed in magic.

FOR SEVERAL HOURS, FIREMEN BATTLED THE FLAMES TO GET THEM under control. Onlookers stood around watching from a safe distance. They moved slowly, as though they'd just come from a very sad funeral, and I saw some of them crying. The rest were numb with disbelief. What began as a quiet winter evening of listening to radios in front of fireplaces had turned into a nightmare.

The campus fire would become an historic event that altered the future for York College, but we didn't know that yet. There was still work to do. Volunteers had to find places to store everything they had dumped outside. Luckily, they had adrenaline to spare. Working side by side, students, faculty members, and townspeople hauled everything to secure places. The book carriers had emptied the library of every volume on the shelves, and they now returned them, with no concern for the Dewey Decimal System.

After the volunteers had sheltered all the rescued items, they hung around, huddled and cold, and asked each other questions like "How did you hear about the fire?" and "What were you doing when you heard about it?" Every personal experience was important, and witnesses felt compelled to share, because nobody could wind down. I thanked God a million times for keeping Denny safe.

The next morning, Denny asked, "Did you ever fall asleep last night? I sure didn't."

"Nope, I rested with my eyes closed but kept replaying everything that happened."

Over our bowls of cornflakes, we talked about the calamity. It still didn't seem real. Rehashing the events helped us accept the reality of what had happened. We found out much later that old electrical wiring had caused the fire.

After breakfast, we wandered across the street to the campus. Swarms of townsfolk had gathered again, that time to witness the rubble in daylight. In the light of a cold sun, the pitiful remains of Old Main, an affectionate term for the Administration Building, brought forth tears from many bystanders. If I'd had the energy, I would've cried, too. A majestic hundred-year-old landmark had gone down. I wondered how it would affect the college.

"Honey, will they replace Old Main?" I asked.

"I doubt they will."

"Why not?"

"They don't have the money to tear it down and build it again."

Businessmen drove up the hill to have a look, probably wondering what effect the tragedy would have on their fair city. York had originally been populated by God-fearing citizens who endorsed a church college in their midst. In the early days, the population grew because no pool hall or tavern was allowed to obtain a business permit, proof to those of faith that families in York, Nebraska, would live in a wholesome environment.

WHILE BUSINESS OWNERS HAD FINANCIAL CONCERNS AFTER THE FIRE, students worried about how they would continue their education. To do that, they needed to attend classes. Denny and other faculty members served on committees that were compelled to find a way to restructure the class schedules. He could hardly eat lunch one day while sharing all the details. "I have no idea how we're going to pull this off. It's not even the end of the first semester."

"What is it you have to do first?" I asked.

He pushed his hands through his hair as though it might pave a clear path for his thoughts. "Well, we're scrambling to find rooms to serve as annexes."

"Whaddya think they'll do?"

"Classes will probably meet wherever there's an open space, even if students have to sit on the floor."

A crude main office was set up in one building and the records office in another. New schedules were posted on a huge bulletin board in the library. The messages changed frequently, and daily life on campus soon revolved around that bulletin board.

"Have you seen the board today?"

"Yes, I checked it at nine o'clock."

"Well, ya better check it again."

"They changed something?"

"Of course they changed something."

A student could read the schedule at 9:00 a.m., go to a class, and find the room empty. On the spur of the moment, administration often switched rooms, and the students just had to keep up. One of the bulletin board messages read:

NOTICE: Residents of Hulitt Hall will be relocated. The bedrooms will become offices.

⚜

WE GOT USED TO THE TURMOIL, AND BEFORE LONG, A CRUDE KIND OF order took shape. It reminded me of my own family. We had changed addresses all too often. I kind of enjoyed relocating and got used to the upheaval, because it felt like camping out in a house. At a young age I often asked, "Mama, when are we moving again?"

Now the question on everyone's mind was, "When will they replace Old Main?" Most people didn't know there was no money to rebuild the structure.

In the meantime, students, faculty, and staff adapted to the primitive setup, and learning resumed. We got used to the remains of a burned-out historical structure in the middle of the campus. Students would slow down, stare, shake their heads sadly, and move on to the library to check the newest announcements. Conversations often began with "before the fire," and January 3, 1951, eventually became a date carved in stone.

The impact of the disaster and the impact of moving on became so intertwined in my mind that I couldn't tell which of the two bothered me the most.

⚜

Chapter 16

Most Representative Woman

T HE FIRE WAS A SOBERING EVENT THAT LEFT EVERYONE CHANGED, but life had to go on. It was my second year at York College, and I had grown up a lot. Although the same person inhabited my body, at twenty-one, I felt older and wiser. The boys had grown up, too. They hadn't played tricks on me in ages, which meant I no longer had to get even with anyone. Most of them found girlfriends, and a few had weddings to plan. For some, the future also meant moving on to graduate school, seminary, or the military.

During our first year of marriage, my husband and I learned to accept our differences. He had entered the world as an organized human being, and I'd arrived with my mother's spontaneous nature. We balanced each other, because he brought order to my life, and I loosened him up a bit.

We valued each other's skills and aptitudes. He admired my singing and artwork. He also liked everything I fed him if you didn't count the "gourmet" dinner I'd cooked with wine. Other than that, he ate whatever I served and asked for seconds. When I invented a recipe with leftovers, he'd say, "That was good. Write it down so you can fix it again." I turned into a good cook because he thought I *was* one.

My husband enlightened me on topics I shied away from, such as history and geography. During the war, he had traveled to foreign countries as a merchant marine. His frightening stories about battles on land and sea made me want to find those places on the map. I imagined Den's fear when he walked through the hold in his ship,

111

checking on the Japanese prisoners, and I visualized the abandoned town his unit discovered, where worthless paper money lay scattered on the ground.

From the beginning of our courtship, I'd thought of Denny as a man of the world. I was provincial, traveling only to a few nearby towns and, once, all the way to Chicago when my mother ran away with us kids. Den, who was born with a compass in his head, taught me which way was north and said, "It's important to know where you're going, especially if your mother is driving." His humor was slightly corny. I often didn't get it but smiled as though I did because I loved him.

Year two at York brought a flurry of activities that sometimes made me dizzy. It felt like living two lives, one as a faculty wife and the other as a student. At faculty functions, I became an actress playing the part of a well-bred, mature young woman. While mingling with students between classes, I let my guard down but never too far. I felt like myself only when we were away from campus, which wasn't very often. Even while alone in our own apartment, we were on the job. The apartment seemed kind of like our office. Playing multiple roles sometimes wore me out, but life wasn't all about me anymore. It was about *us*.

It took a while, but my husband and I also got used to each other's quirks. I took my time with homework but breezed through housework. To help me finish homework on time, Denny often bailed me out of housework. He did a better job of vacuuming the floor and dusting the furniture than I, though he took forever. When I said, "Honey, you don't have to work so hard at it," he said, "I don't mind. I'm just getting the spots you missed." He was a perfectionist, so I learned to accept my husband's need to clean what I'd already cleaned.

Like other young married couples, we worried about money. My husband's teaching paycheck of $209 a month couldn't possibly pay for all of our expenses. He moonlighted on weekends as an official for sports events to help make ends meet, but our budget was still tight.

Over and over again, he asked for a salary advance from Helen Jo Polk, the treasurer. She cautioned him by saying, "You realize these advances mean that each month's paycheck will be smaller than it's supposed to be?"

Yes, Denny knew that, and he worried. Long before we met, he'd held down three jobs at a time to put himself through college. Now his goal to finish a master's degree and go straight into doctoral studies meant finding a school that offered graduate fellowships where he could teach while attending classes. His initiative made me proud.

My goals were easier to obtain. I wanted to graduate and get pregnant, and not necessarily in that order. When a woman starts daydreaming about having a baby, she's slightly nuts, and that's all she can think about. Well, that was me, crazy for a baby. Den said, "Now calm down, Betty. We can't afford children yet. I have to finish school."

When I heard that, my heart fell. I could be as old as twenty-five, or maybe even twenty-six, before getting pregnant, and Denny would be over thirty. That seemed so old. How could I possibly wait that long?

If our near future didn't include a baby, I could at least practice being domestic. In between thinking in French, as my instructor suggested, and writing papers for my literature class, I thought about planting a garden. Some of my sweetest memories were about my brother, sister, and me working in our Victory Gardens during the war. I also wanted to start sewing again. Making my own clothes cost less than buying them. I'd learned how to use my mother's old-fashioned treadle machine at the age of eleven and sewed my own clothes once I got to high school. I decided to put together a really nice outfit for an all-student banquet we would soon attend. But I had no sewing machine. My husband said, "The perfect place to buy one is at Dirty Dick Dean's store."

"Where?"

He explained the nickname. He had played football at York with Richard Dean, who didn't bother to shower after practice, and that bad habit labeled him.

"Is that the name of his store?"

"No. It's called Dean's Used Furniture, but everyone in town remembers his old name."

At Dirty Dick Dean's shop, I found an old Singer treadle like Mom's for twelve dollars and asked how much it would cost for delivery. He said, "Five extra dollars for that service," so I paid him seventeen dollars, thankful that he now smelled clean and fragrant.

The anticipation of owning a sewing machine thrilled me, and I couldn't wait to get started. After setting it up, Denny left for school. I drove to the fabric store downtown. Once through the door, the familiar scent of cut-rate cloth washed over me, causing a nostalgia attack. I hovered forever over the pages of each pattern catalogue. There were too many to choose from: McCall, Simplicity, Butterick, and Vogue.

A Simplicity pattern caught my eye. What made it stylish was a removable peplum, a skirt-like flare attached to a band that wrapped around the waist and fastened in front. Then a lime green and white print got my attention. It required lime green thread to match. Our scissors at home couldn't cut paper, so I added a pair of Wiss shears to my purchases. Next I bought a package of straight pins, bringing the total bill to almost seven dollars. Yikes! I could've bought ready-made for that price. I didn't care. I wanted the fun of using my new/old sewing machine.

I loved each step of constructing a garment, and every dart, seam, and ruffle turned into an art project. My mother taught me to think that way about any job. She had problems but also had a noble side that helped a person overlook the other part. For Mom, good craftsmanship meant the inside of your garment had to be as perfect as the outside. We both loved the process of construction more than the finished project.

Denny and I took our time with projects, too, and didn't slap things together the way I rushed through housework. For that reason, I should've started my dress project earlier. Buying a sewing machine, doing homework, purchasing supplies, and studying pattern directions had eaten up the time. In a rush, I spread everything on the kitchen table to make it easy to pin pattern pieces where they belonged and start cutting. Then I basted, sewed, pressed, and tried on the almost-finished dress. The inside was not perfect. The outside wasn't either.

With only two hours left before the banquet started and no full-length mirror, I viewed my reflection in the window. The design had looked attractive in the catalog, but the glass reflected an image of me in a costume with a very fluffy waistline. I didn't want to be seen in public wearing it and yelled into the next room. "Honey, this thing tonight … do we have to attend?"

"Betty, we don't *have* to attend anything; we're *encouraged* to attend."

"So, how important is tonight's event?"

"Fairly important."

"Why?"

He stopped his work to join me in the kitchen. "Let me think a minute. Well, it's a banquet honoring two students, the male and female who best represent the student body." Then he looked closely at me and asked, "Are you wearing *that*?"

"Yeah, but I don't like it."

"I don't either. Wear something else."

I had nothing else nice to wear. My clothes were meant for school. I convinced him to let me alter it, even though we'd get to the banquet a little late. I slashed out great chunks of fabric, removed most of the flare on the peplum, and sewed it back up. By then, we'd missed the banquet. He said, "You look okay, so let's go."

While we were sneaking in, someone saw us and asked, "Where have you guys been? The program was supposed to start fifteen minutes ago."

Denny said, "I don't understand."

"Didn't anyone tell you?

"Tell me what?"

"The faculty chose Betty as Most Representative Woman for 1951."

I nearly choked. Nobody had informed us about the award. The stranger led me to the stage, where I sat on a chair covered in satin cloth, wearing my dippy dress. If anyone had told me I'd be on display, I would've purchased a nice outfit at Montgomery Wards. Was I thrilled with the honor? No. I was 100 percent fixated on my clothing instead. What a nerve-wracking experience. Johnnie Mann, a straight-arrow future minister guy, had been named Most Representative Man for 1951. He took his rightful place on the other satin-draped chair, and we beamed fake smiles for snapshots.

Thank goodness they took the important yearbook photos in a studio a few days later. My hubby helped me find a more appropriate garment for that occasion.

I never understood why the faculty chose me as Most Representative Woman. *Imposter* would've been a better title, since I felt uncertain about my faith while living there. What did I represent? I was baffled, but Denny was not. Pride caused him to beam the way men do when their team wins a game.

It wasn't easy, but I put the troubling thoughts aside and accepted the honor with grace.

Betty, Most Representative Woman 1951

CHAPTER 17

After the Fire

CAMPUS ACTIVITIES HAD TO TAKE A BACK SEAT SO WE COULD FOCUS on our plans for the future. Before the fire, Denny had been pondering how to afford a doctorate. If he could teach at Colorado State College of Education in Greeley while going to school and I got a job, we could manage. His graduate record was excellent, so he mailed an application for a fellowship and crossed his fingers for luck. I didn't need to cross my fingers. I felt certain he'd qualify for a fellowship. As a backup plan, I prayed really hard.

A few weeks later, a special delivery letter launched us into the next chapter in our lives. That letter included the contract we'd been hoping for, proof that crossing fingers and praying pay off.

My husband's assignment meant starting classes for his advanced degree in the fall of 1951 while teaching math at the campus high school. We still had to find a place to live, and unbeknownst to us, the woman in charge of the fellowship contract had taken care of that, too. She called and introduced herself as Dr. Grace Wilson, asking to speak with Denny Auchard.

I said, "Dr. Wilson, the Dean of Women?"

"Yes, that used to be my job."

"Three years ago, you and my principal at Englewood High School helped with a tuition waiver for my first year of college. I was Betty Peal. Do you remember me?"

"Yes, I do remember you. How remarkable that our paths have crossed again. You must be Denny's wife."

"I am. I'll put him on the phone."

Why would she contact my husband? After handing him the phone, I thought about the day Mr. Eugene Gullette had called me to his office when he discovered that I had no plans to continue my education after graduation. I told him my parents wanted me to find a job because they couldn't afford any more schooling. He'd said, "Let's see what I can do about that." He grabbed the phone, dialed, and pushed his palm toward me as a sign to wait. Then he said, "Hi, Grace. This is Gene. I need your help for a student." Because of his intervention for a tuition waver, I was able to attend college.

As Denny talked with Dr. Wilson, I watched his expression first reveal curiosity and then amazement. However, I wasn't really listening. My mind became so lost in memories that I heard only the end of his conversation when he said, "Thank you so much, Grace, and we'll call as soon as we arrive. Bye."

"Honey, what was that about?"

He still had that amazed look on his face when he said "Listen to this. We're going to be dorm supervisors again."

"What?"

"Just listen. We can't afford to turn this down. We'll have a furnished apartment in Gordon Hall on the campus, and a maid will clean the place every week. We'll be houseparents for thirty-six girls. We'll eat dinner in the dining hall every night with young women from four dorms."

"Oh, my gosh. I ate there three times a day during my freshman year."

My husband couldn't stop. "We won't pay rent, and we won't have to buy gasoline very often, because everything is within walking distance. Betty, how much better can this get?"

So many wonderful things happening at once didn't seem real. Our move away from York would be a happy event instead of a sad one.

It wasn't all happy, though. When we found out that we couldn't take Chipper to our new job, someone on the faculty volunteered to adopt her. When he and his wife came to pick her up, I hugged her and had a serious girl-to-girl talk about being a good dog for her new family. Her worried expression meant she knew something was up, and it caused my lower lip to quiver. The quiver turned into all-out sobbing when I saw her face and paws pressed against the car window as they drove away. My sadness at having to give up our puppy hovered around me for days.

Carl had earned his credential and would be teaching history in the high school at Dannebrog, Nebraska. They would take Doggie with them. As happy as I was for them, a little jealousy crept in, but I never told Carl and Glenna how I felt. Before they left York, we got together to celebrate, not with forbidden wine but with homemade root beer floats on the house.

We spread the word of our move to Colorado by way of a few relatives who developed a telephone tree to let everyone else know. Daily, we received congratulatory calls from people wanting to know the details. One of those calls came from my mother in Denver. She said, "I'm sure happy about your move closer to home, but where will you live?" After we chatted about our plans, she changed the subject, saying, "I have some good and bad news." I hated that line. "The good stuff first: Your Aunt Lora, at the age of thirty-seven, finally found a husband." I already knew that but didn't say so; Mom didn't like being interrupted. "Her husband seems real nice, even though he's older and has been married before." I had no idea where Mom picked up that kind of information. "Anyway, they had a lovely church gathering, and I think the entire Peal clan attended."

"Mom, I'm glad to hear this."

She jumped back in. "This next news will shock you." That scared me. My mother paused and took a deep breath before continuing. "The night of Lora's wedding, your Uncle Paul took his own life."

"Oh, no, Mom."

"Yes, he did. He sat in the car in the closed garage with the motor turned on."

Memories flooded my thoughts. In the eighth grade I had lived with Aunt Edith and Uncle Paul for a few weeks when my family had to split up while Dad looked for a place to rent. I'd enjoyed my time with them and felt like one of their children while staying there.

I thanked my mother for letting me know, but the bad news ruined my excitement about moving.

WE'D BEEN PACKING IN A FLURRY SO WE COULD HIT THE ROAD FOR Greeley early the next morning. Stowing our belongings and cleaning the apartment took longer than expected, and early the next morning became later the next evening. Our new Pontiac bulged with boxes and suitcases, with barely enough room for my feet. My family had moved that way many times when I was growing up, so the chaos was familiar.

Around 7:00 p.m., Denny locked the Thompson Hall doors, and we crawled over the boxes in our car. He started the motor and said, "Well, Betty, here we go. Are you ready?"

I didn't have time to answer before another vehicle pulled alongside. The passenger rolled down the window and said, "What's your hurry?" Heavens to Betsy, it was Aunt Lora, the bride. She asked, "Where are you two going?"

"We're moving to Colorado."

"We're on our honeymoon and just dropped by to say hello. Before you leave, I'd like you to meet my husband, Harold Bordwell. "

I waved and said, "Hi, Harold."

"I'm also delivering a package from Kathleen.'

"From Aunt Kathleen?"

"Yes, it's your belated wedding present."

Denny sighed and turned off the motor. After hauling ourselves out of the car, we returned to the living room to chat with Lora and her groom.

We opened the gift to find a pair of hand-painted wooden Pennsylvania Dutch plates Aunt Kathleen had made. It touched me. Then my aunt approached a new subject with caution. "Umm … speakin' of gifts, did you ever receive the set of aluminum pans I sent?"

Embarrassment turned my cheeks red. I hadn't sent a thank-you card, and it had been two years since our marriage. I apologized too many times and told her how often we used our cooking pans. She brushed it aside to bring up the topic of the family tragedy. "Betty, did ya hear what your Uncle Paul did?" I told her Mom had called. I dreaded talking about the horrific subject, but my aunt needed to get it off her chest and continued. "How could he do such a thing on my wedding day?"

Harold, the new husband, listened with patience as his wife droned on, apparently sensing he shouldn't jump in. She said, "Paul must've been outta his mind to choose that day t' end it all." I nodded and stayed as quiet as Harold and Denny, but she couldn't stop. "Now, on every anniversary, I won't have happy memories. Instead, I'll be thinkin' about that awful, awful thing he did."

Anyone who knew Uncle Paul grieved, shocked by the heartbreak of his bewildering death. For a long time, he had suffered from depression over losing his nine-year-old son to leukemia. He might've temporarily lost his mind, and I felt both pity and revulsion. I couldn't handle any more talk about the tragedy.

My aunt's drop-in visit soon turned into an intolerable situation. In addition to other painful subjects, she reminded me that I took my first steps to *her* and not to my mother. I knew she had always disliked Mom for running away now and then, but I had put those memories away a long time ago. Hearing her dredge them up once again was almost more than I could tolerate. For an hour, I endured her unwelcome presence as she recalled various Peal family problems. Finally, she ran out of unpleasant topics and said, "Well, we'd better get on with our honeymoon." I heartily agreed.

We hugged goodbye and went our separate ways. Aunt Lora and Harold, my new uncle, drove into their future as Mr. and Mrs. Bordwell, where they'd create their own memories. Denny and I would do the same as houseparents to thirty-six girls in a college dormitory. Supervising so many young women would have to take the place of becoming *real* parents ... at least for a while.

Union Colony Apartments

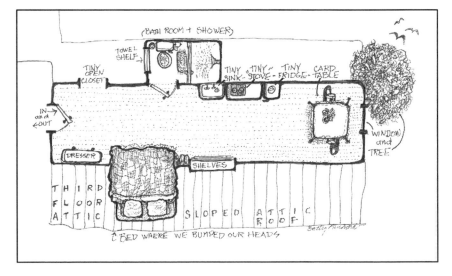

Union Colony Floor Plan

Chapter 18

Blessed with Good Luck

Before I met Denny, I was a freshman at Colorado State College of Education in Greeley. I took long walks on campus for several reasons: to put off my homework; to avoid learning to play bridge, which college students seemed to love; and to explore the surrounding neighborhoods. That's when I discovered an enormous multistory home that sat on a rise above the corner of 10th Avenue and 17th Street. The huge structure reigned like a queen over all the cottages in the neighborhood. I often wondered who owned it. Obviously, only a wealthy family would live in a place the size of a ship.

I had no idea I would soon live there.

A few years later, I learned that the college had purchased the building. They named it Union Colony Apartments and rented furnished units to married college students. Before leaving York, we had reserved apartment 303 by phone, sight unseen, because we had to stay somewhere during July and August. That was all the time Denny needed to prepare for his oral exams. At the end of August, we would pack up our simple belongings and relocate to begin our new job as houseparents in a girls' dorm.

Moving three times in a short period promised to be exhilarating. Our future looked good, and my insides were so full of smiles that I felt chubby.

When we set eyes on unit 303, we didn't know whether to laugh or cry. We settled on laughter because it was easier. Our new temporary home had a far-fetched floor plan consisting of a twenty-foot corridor with a cubicle on the left side that housed the bathroom and a space on the right for a bed.

The bed was a mere thirty-five inches below the roof. We kept forgetting where we were sleeping. Each morning, we'd throw off the covers, sit up, and bump our heads on the sloped ceiling. We must've whacked ourselves stupid a hundred times. My husband said, "I'm gonna be brain damaged before taking my orals."

Living in our crowded corridor reminded me of playing house in my grandmother's attic. We cooked simple meals on a two-burner gas stove that had four short legs. The stove sat on a ledge instead of the floor, and we had no oven. The cute refrigerator that stood as high as my waist turned out to be the perfect place to set the dark green fan Den had rescued from the fire. Nobody had claimed the heavy, old, ugly thing, but it worked, so we kept it.

A wobbly card table with a couple of folding chairs claimed a place next to the attic window. We ate meals there and watched the world go by three stories below. Tree branches brushed the screen, and the view made it seem like camping in a tree house. That end of the living space became my favorite spot.

Den and I became friends with Claude and Anna Schmitz, who lived in 302, a "standard" unit. Claude, who went by the nickname Schmitty, had a wondrous tenor voice and had sung professionally in New York, but he longed to be a teacher. While her husband worked on his doctorate in music, Anna worked in the library. They'd been dying to compare apartments. After a tour of the twenty feet from our door to the window, I could tell they were stifling either laughter or shock in an effort to avoid hurting our feelings. When they invited us to have iced tea in *their* apartment, we could stand up straight everywhere. Their ceiling was clearly better than our ceiling. In spite of my envy, we grew very close to Claude and Anna.

We also befriended Hank and Marty, a young couple on the second floor. He had a job in town, and she was studying for her teacher's credential. Unfortunately, Marty got polio and ended up in the hospital. The residents of Union Colony were like family, so we helped Hank by making meals for him. When his wife finally returned home and had to stay in bed, we pitched in to help feed her, too. A few weeks later, Fern, another woman who lived in the building, came down with sleeping sickness.

Word got around that two other couples in the house were so afraid of catching one of these maladies that they moved away. Den and I had been blessed with good luck and didn't worry a twit about catching polio, sleeping sickness, or anything else going around.

AS PLANNED, MY HUSBAND SPENT MOST OF THAT SUMMER PREPARING for his master's degree oral exams. His flair for mathematics, my most feared subject, put me in awe of his intelligence. Just the thought of taking an oral test in arithmetic caused my blood to run cold.

He reviewed everything he'd ever learned about advanced mathematics so he would pass with high marks, and I helped by reading from a long list of questions that he practiced answering. During all the questioning and answering, the only thing I learned about mathematics was that it was over my head. No surprise there.

The evening before the big day, he said, "Let's go to the movies."

"Tonight? Shouldn't you keep studying?"

"Nope. If I forget about it for a while, I'll feel more relaxed."

We saw *Annie Get Your Gun*, a perfect film for getting your mind off exams.

His orals started at ten o'clock the next morning. He sat up, bumped his head on the ceiling, flopped back down, and said, "I just knocked everything I knew about math out of my brain."

"Oh, no! I hope you're kidding."

I made a mental note to move the pillows to the other end of the bed, where there was a little more headspace.

After pulling himself together, he ate a bowl of Shredded Wheat and left for a few hours. When he strutted back through the door, beaming, I said, "You're finished already?"

"I'm finished, and you won't believe how much fun I had."

"Fun? How could you possibly call a math test fun?"

"Betty, it's hard to explain. I'd taken classes from the four professors, so they knew me. It was more like a conversation about the pure science of mathematics than a test."

"What did they ask you?"

"They took turns asking me to elaborate on certain mathematical concepts. I really enjoyed explaining each topic, pretending they knew nothing about the subject."

"Did you pass?"

"With high marks."

Each successful step toward our future filled me with confidence. With Denny at the helm, we would never be as poor as either of our families.

CHAPTER 19

Denny's Ready

OUR NEW POSITION AS HOUSEPARENTS IN A GIRLS' DORM IN Greeley included a bonus that any young wife would drool over. I had to pinch myself to make sure it was real.

As dorm supervisors, we would eat dinner every evening at Tobey-Kendall, the dining hall next to our building. Eating out every night would make the job seem like a vacation, because food tasted a million times better when someone else cooked it. While living in that hot attic, we'd melted away a few ounces every day, which accumulated to a loss of several pounds for each of us. I knew we'd gain back every ounce soon after we moved to the dorm. Did I care about gaining back lost weight? Not a bit. I intended to enjoy every meal.

BEFORE WE MOVED INTO OUR NEW HOME IN SEPTEMBER, A COLLEGE administrator arranged for us to meet with the previous dorm parents so they could show us around and explain our responsibilities. I recognized the couple from my freshman year. I also remembered that Dr. Hollenberg was the grumpy guy who'd yelled at us the previous summer for parking in a no-parking zone. Denny didn't seem to be aware, so when I had a chance, I whispered, "You know who that man is, don't you?" He looked again and then raised his eyebrows while slowly nodding yes. We made the connection, but the professor didn't. What a strange feeling it was to fake cordiality while wanting to punch him in the nose.

We smiled and nodded as they gave us a tour of our new apartment. Compared to the used furniture in Thompson Hall, Gordon Hall furnishings seemed brand new. The matching bedroom set included the bed, two nightstands with lamps, a dressing table and bench, a mirror, and a huge chest of drawers. The living room featured a lovely emerald velvet couch, a matching overstuffed chair and ottoman, and a small library table with a chair. Neither Denny nor I had grown up with anything that fancy.

The residents of Gordon Hall ranged from brand new freshman to upperclassmen returning from summer break. Some of them appeared to be disappointed the Hollenbergs had left, and others seemed glad. Our job was to earn the support of all the residents. We would be there for only a year and wanted to keep things normal, whatever "normal" might be. For me, it meant not rocking the boat and handling any issues with a light touch.

A senior who knew the ropes helped us welcome the rest. I think she was trying to please Denny. Women, young and old, always spoke to him before noticing I was there, too. It didn't bother me that his good looks and modest manner had that effect. In fact, I loved it! Everyone liked my husband so much I assumed they automatically would like me.

He helped the girls stash suitcases and trunks in the basement storage area, and they soon got to know him well. I couldn't help but say, "You sure got a better welcome here than I got at Thompson Hall."

We crammed to learn the dormitory rules and regulations by heart. If we appeared to be knowledgeable and confident, I assumed everything would go smoothly. As soon as all thirty-six students settled in, we held our first meeting, sharing the podium so they would see us as a team. Within the week, they were calling us Mr. and Mrs. A. My nickname stuck, and twenty years later my students used it when I taught art in high school.

As DORM PARENTS, WE WERE SUPPOSED TO STICK TO THE 10:00 P.M. curfew by turning off porch lights and locking the front door. But we were dyed-in-the-wool softies, locking and unlocking the door to let young women in who had necked too long in the parking lot. Denny said, "We shoulda started out strict, because this is getting old." I agreed 100 percent. He came up with a plan. "This is what I'm gonna do. At the next weekly meeting, I'm telling them that their necking time interferes with *our* necking time."

"No, hon … don't say that!"

"Betty, I'm kidding. But I'll warn them that if they don't honor the curfew, I will personally go out to the parking lot and start knocking on car windows."

What irony. We were still dealing with the heavy petters, just as we had done in Thompson Hall, but this time Den had to do the dirty work.

Our job was uncomplicated and fairly stress free, which allowed Den to start his doctoral classes and a dissertation with ease. His fellowship would provide financial security for a year. We lived and worked on a beautiful campus, adorned with blocks of green grass, handsome architecture, and trees taller than the buildings. My favorite building housed the melodic tower chimes. I almost fell into a meditative state when counting the tones to check the time of day.

Even though Greeley looked beautiful, it often smelled bad. When the wind blew our direction, the city reeked of manure, thanks to the Monfort Feedlots in the countryside. Residents had grown so used to the smell that they never pinched their noses or said "peeyoo" the way we did. Since we were the only people complaining, we soon pretended not to notice the odor of cow poop in the air.

✦

ONE DAY, MY HUBBY SAID, "BETTY, MY FELLOWSHIP ENDS NEXT YEAR. Then I'll have to find a teaching job."

"Yeah, I know. Are you worried about it?"

"No, not at all. I just think we shouldn't wait 'til I finish school to make a baby."

"Are you serious?"

"I am."

I gave it some thought for three seconds and said, "Alrighty then. Let's do it."

"Betty, I don't mean this very minute. I mean let's stop trying *not* to get pregnant."

"Okay, we'll stop trying not to get pregnant. When?"

Den thought about it for two seconds and asked, "How about tonight?"

CHAPTER 20

Making Change

OUR DECISION TO START A FAMILY RIGHT AWAY ADDED A GLOW TO my complexion. Soon I would be a real mother instead of a housemother to college students. Picturing myself as a parent occupied most of my thoughts.

Denny didn't daydream. He was a worker bee with three major assignments: teaching math in the campus high school, excelling in his graduate classes, and ... *now* ... making a baby. He rarely expressed feelings in words and kept his emotions inside. No words were necessary for me to read his state of mind. The spring in his step and day-to-day smiles said, "I like what I'm doing."

My husband excelled in subjects that my brain rejected. If conversations turned to topics such as percent, interest, or math of any kind, I didn't have much to say. I excelled in other areas, such as drawing, acting, and singing. In my freshman year at Greeley, I sang with a trio every week on the college radio station and acted in the weekly radio show *Wings for the Martins*. I played the part of Mrs. Martin. Nobody in Greeley had encountered the full spectrum of my personality, because I hadn't shown all my colors.

I filled my days by experimenting with recipes for two, reading, and visiting with Gladys, the housekeeper. The girls in the dorm dashed in and out so fast I had no chance to get to know them very well. My duty was to turn off the porch lights at 10:01 p.m. every night and lock the front door. Anyone could do it. I thought about taking a class but decided to find a second job instead. Montgomery Ward, which my family called "Monkey Wards," had an opening for a clerk.

I said, "Honey, I want to be a salesgirl."

Denny looked skeptical. "Do you know how to use a cash register?"

"No, but they can teach me."

"Do you know how to make change?"

"Of course."

THE STORE HIRED ME AS SOON AS I APPLIED, SO OFF I WENT TO WOMen's clothing on the second floor. The first half of the day, I shadowed my boss as she explained everything I should know for completing a sale. She made it look easy. I figured chitchatting with customers would be way more fun than cleaning up after twelve boys in Thompson Hall.

After lunch, she said, "Now it's your turn to be the salesgirl."

I showed real talent for the chitchat part, as I helped ladies decide what looked nice on them and what didn't. They appreciated my input. They didn't appreciate how long it took me to figure out what they owed and how much money they should receive back. I scribbled the figures on a piece of paper when I needed to subtract the cost of the item from the money they'd handed me. It reminded me of the confusion I'd felt in fifth-grade arithmetic when we had to come up with the solution to a complex story problem.

All afternoon, sweat covered my brow and soaked the armpits of my blouse. Working with numbers used the slow part of my brain, the left side, and that's why it took so long. When a customer glared at the coins I'd dropped in her hand and said, "You've shortchanged me ten dollars," I knew it was over for me.

My kindhearted trainer helped straighten it out and said, "Betty, don't worry. You'll get the hang of it."

I would never get the hang of it, but somehow I got through the rest of the shift. When the store closed at nine, I headed straight to the manager's office and turned myself in. He was so sympathetic and gentle that he allowed me to babble on and on until I ended with an apology, saying, "I'm sorry that I'm not good at this. I need to quit."

He smiled and said, "That's a wise decision. I would've let you go, and you don't want that on your record." I thanked him and left with the word *record* hanging over my head like a cartoon caption in a balloon. It wasn't Monkey Wards talk; it was police talk.

※

THAT NIGHT I TOLD DENNY MY SAD STORY, AND HE SAID, "I THOUGHT you knew how to make change."

"Honey, I thought I did, too, but all that subtracting with everyone looking over my shoulder while I did the math on scraps of paper made me nervous."

"Subtracting? You subtracted?"

"Of course I subtracted."

"Betty, when returning change, you're *adding* instead of subtracting."

To be honest, that sounded crazy.

He said, "We should've practiced before you applied."

I loved my husband but didn't want him to be my teacher.

"Denny, if I learned how to handle money, I could end up wasting my skills, and I do have some skills. It's too late to practice. I'm looking for a different kind of work."

※

MY NEXT EMPLOYMENT LANDED ME IN THE COLLEGE ACQUISITIONS department, which was housed in the college library basement. It required opening packages from publishers, placing the invoices inside each book, and stacking the books on a cart. Another employee then wheeled the cart to the office that paid bills. I made a note to myself to never apply for a job in the bill-paying department.

Catherine, an adorable, white-haired fairy godmother, was the acquisitions supervisor. She was so lighthearted that my responsibilities felt more like play than work. It took no special skills to be employed in her department. However, other employees might not have enjoyed reading new book titles as much as I did.

※

With our working lives settled, Denny and I discovered a social life and a church at the same time. After visiting our former places of worship, the Missouri Synod Lutheran and the Evangelical United Brethren, we opted for something new of our own choosing. We felt most at home with the Presbyterians, who had an inquisitive and broadminded pastor and several organizations for adults of all ages. We joined the young married couples in the Mariners Club. Married couples aged fifty and older were referred to as the Ancient Mariners. Singles were adults of any age who didn't have a mate but played well with others. They had more fun than any of us.

At twenty-five and twenty-one, we were the youngest in our group. We gravitated toward an older couple of thirty-five years of age. Jim and Arlyce monitored articulate and lively discussion groups. She had already "caught" pregnancy, a condition I hoped to catch soon, which gave us a lot to talk about. Our husbands were seeking doctorate degrees in education, with mine focused on counseling and guidance and hers on history. Denny had grown up as a preacher's kid in the Bible belt during Dust Bowl days and prohibition. His stories were living history, which gave the two men plenty to discuss.

With Jim and Arlyce in charge, club members conversed about spiritual topics such as why we choose one faith over another. Jim said, "With my various teaching assignments and schooling, Arlyce and I move a lot. For that reason, we attend wherever our spiritual needs are met, because we're both broadminded."

I'd never experienced such a casual approach to religion before. In my catechism class, the minister emphasized that only Missouri Synod members would go to heaven. For most of my senior year, I believed him. The Mariners discussion group leaned toward a broader approach to the subject of believing. Their consensus: there is no right or wrong way to believe. We have choices.

That point of view sounded almost sacrilegious, but it also seemed reasonable. The church had influenced me during a vulnerable stage of life, my teen years. As an adult, conversations with truth seekers from various backgrounds who held unique philosophical opinions no longer confused me. Instead, I felt liberated. My new way of thinking fit as comfortably as an old coat. Arlyce introduced another concept when she said, "God is many things to different people. For the Native Americans, all things in nature represent God. Some of my friends from India believe that God is in us all, and we are God."

That idea appealed to me more than any we'd discussed, even though I was afraid to say so out loud. I could imagine someone whispering behind her hand to a friend, "Did Betty say what I think she said?"

"Yep. She thinks she's God."

I joined the discussions without guilt, and Denny brought a lot to the table, as well, which surprised me. His religious upbringing, like mine, embraced unbending rules and strict doctrine. We talked about our new direction a lot. One day, he said, "Betty, if our families could see us now, what would they say?"

"Hon, let's face it. We're converting to a faith called Born-Again Thinkers."

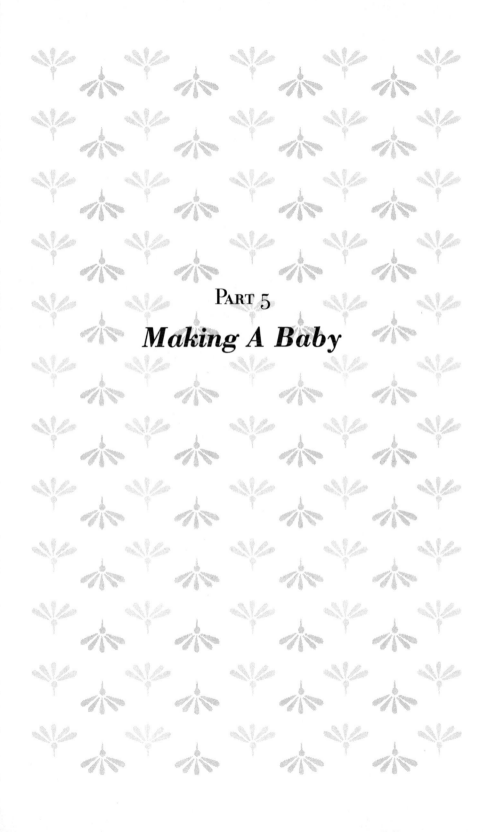

PART 5

Making A Baby

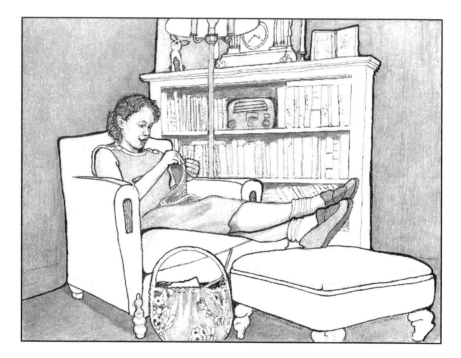

Betty Knits and Waits

Chapter 21

Passing Time

Denny stayed hunched over his desk that summer, working on graduate assignments and leaving me to act as the Gordon Hall supervisor. On my own, I had to deal with a flurry of students moving in and out. It created a mix of nervousness and nostalgia. Usually, he and I ran the show together, and this changing of the guard meant I needed to know what I was doing ... or at least look like it. I felt slightly overwhelmed, because the place resembled a busy bus station. New students transferred from other colleges for summer session, and others stayed in our dorm but changed rooms. To keep track of all the comings and goings, I said goodbye to some and hello to others. It became so confusing that I once said goodbye to a young woman who had just arrived. After a couple of days, the hustle bustle ended. The girls were in place and ready for classes to begin.

Den came up for air and asked, "Well, dorm mother, how did it go?"

I wanted to avoid confessing that without his support I'd started out nervous, so I waved the air as he often did and said, "Couldn'ta been easier." Pretending it had been easy made it seem true. And it *was* sort of true, because I could feel my confidence growing.

I soon felt so at ease with the residents that when I smelled a mouthwatering aroma a few weeks after we arrived, I bounced into the kitchen to see what was going on. Laura Nakasuji, a tall, beautiful Japanese senior, was forming rice balls. Then I caught a glimpse of dark, glistening strips of meat in the frying pan. Almost drooling, I said, "Wow. I am dying for a taste of that!"

She smiled and used a fork to snag a piece, which I popped into my mouth. Succulent beef and a rich, salty-sweet sauce coated my tongue, rendering me nearly speechless. I groaned and managed to say, "This is wonderful."

"Mrs. A, you'd enjoy our luau."

"What's a luau?"

"It's a Hawaiian picnic with pineapples, raw fish, poi, and a whole pig that we roast underground for two days. You and Mr. A are invited."

Even though I'd never heard of a luau and the menu sounded weird, I accepted on the spot.

Another epicurean event on campus was the International Food Fair. It opened my eyes to many marvelous gastronomic creations from around the world. The Italian booth offered samples of pizza pie, something else that was new to me. I rushed to get in line, expecting an Italian version of apple pie. Instead, I was treated to melted cheese over sausage and tomatoes on a thin crust. Pizza pie ... what a marvelous invention. I wondered if such delicacies were brand new to everyone, or if I'd been living in a cave. I'd had no reason to travel beyond my own little world, but all of a sudden my world seemed larger than ever.

IN ADDITION TO ENJOYING SUMMERTIME PLEASURES ELSEWHERE ON campus, I got better acquainted with the Gordon Hall housekeeper. Gladys kept me laughing. Her gangly frame was put together as loose and floppy as her dust rag, and her personality was delightful. She worked in our building twice a week, moving methodically from the top floor to ground level and cleaning with such ease that it seemed she'd been doing it all her life. A container of supplies and a vacuum cleaner, the tools of her trade, must have been attached to her hip, because they seemed to go with her everywhere. Our apartment was last on her tour of duty. During cleaning sessions, I discovered her curious vernacular. Gladys used words that sounded like the real thing but weren't. One afternoon, she said, "Mrs. A, my legs ache all the time. Since the girls can't see me, is it all right if I sit down in your living room for just a few minutes?"

I said, "Take more than a few minutes, Gladys. I'll bring in some iced tea, and we can chat while I knit."

"Oh, no. If I'm caught sittin' on the job for too long, I'll get canned."

"Okay, but what's wrong with your legs?"

"They hurt, and I hafta wear special stockings."

"Special stockings? Why?"

"I got very close veins."

It took a few seconds to realize she meant *varicose* veins.

I planned to make a list of her almost-right terms but failed to do so. Instead, I carried her terminology in my head and shared it with Denny so we could add color to our boring vocabulary. I felt great affection for Gladys. She was sincere, earnest, and good-hearted, a bright spot in my life. When my husband and I used those words, I always thought of her.

FOR SOME REASON, THE SUMMER SCHOOL STUDENTS SEEMED A BIT different from those attending the regular sessions. For example, they honored the curfew without being reminded. I had no idea why. When I'd been a freshman in Snyder Hall, our housemother, Mrs. G (for Glidden) enforced the rule with no mercy. I never tested her, but rumor had it that when 10:00 p.m. arrived, she opened the door for no one. A story spread about a tardy freshman who'd been locked out and had to find her own way in. She knocked on a first-floor dorm window and asked a student she didn't even know to please let her in by the fire escape exit on the second floor. It might've been a story Mrs. G. herself started to scare her charges into following the rules.

We were too wimpy to lock *anyone* out and enforced the curfew our own way.

SUMMER FLEW BY WITH A FLURRY OF MEMORABLE EVENTS, BUT THE most important happened in August. Denny and I were wide-eyed with excitement because I had missed my first period. I called Dr. Barber with the good news. He said, "Betty, it's too soon to be sure. Call me again in a couple of months." My heart fell. "We'll give you a frog test then to confirm pregnancy."

"How can a frog tell if I'm pregnant?"

"Well, the test requires two things: a *Xenopus laevis* female and a urine sample from you."

"Dr. Barber, are you kidding?"

"No. That's the truth. A lab technician injects your urine into the creature's dorsal lymph sac; if you're pregnant, she lays eggs twelve hours later. No eggs, no pregnancy, which reminds me that I need to see if they've run out of frogs."

"What happens when they don't have a frog on hand?"

"They have more shipped from Africa."

I couldn't believe I had to wait sixty days for confirmation even though I was positive I had finally gotten pregnant. I didn't need a frog to prove it. I wanted to broadcast the news to everyone, but Den said, "No, let's wait."

Time passed as though it had nowhere to go, and I was desperate for something to do. They didn't need me at the library, so I took up knitting again. It was more fun to knit while chatting, so I spent many hours in the dormitory reception room and visited with anyone in the mood to talk. Since I didn't know the gender of our baby, I purchased aqua-colored yarn for a sweater and booties. A student saw me working on the booties and asked, "Mrs. A, who's having a baby?"

"My cousin in Iowa."

I've told some lies in my life but none as quickly as that one.

AT HOME, MY HUSBAND WAS USUALLY SO BUSY TYPING THAT WE RARELY engaged in casual chitchat. I sometimes entertained myself by watching his fingers fly across the keys as easily as my mother's did when she played the piano. Of course, he produced words instead of music. While I hadn't learned to play the piano, I figured I could learn how to type. When winter quarter started, I enrolled in a typing class on campus.

I loved practicing the exercises. The letters *g h f j d k s l* skipped off my fingertips like eight little tap dancers. When Den got to our typewriter first, I had to practice on the tabletop, and sometimes my fingers tripped over each other, because there were no keys to touch. When I tripped up in the classroom, it happened because I typed too fast trying to impress my instructor. He said, "Betty, typing is not a race. Keep a slow and steady pace."

A slow and steady pace had been my motto for a few months, and I begrudged it. When my third missed period approached, I experienced a huge sense of relief. After my breasts grew tender, I couldn't stop smiling and said, "Honey, I'm sure Dr. Barber will confirm my pregnancy soon."

"I hope he remembered to order a frog."

"Yeah, so do I, but I want to tell people now. I can't stand waiting."

"Betty, just use the time to get better at typing."

And that's what I did. But being patient wasn't easy.

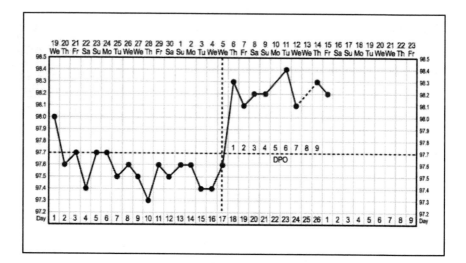

The Scientific Method

CHAPTER 22

The Scientific Method

I MADE A SUPREME EFFORT TO AVOID BEING RESTLESS WHILE WAITING for the test that would make my pregnancy official. I set knitting needles aside and threw myself into helping our Mariners Club raise money for church projects. We came up with all kinds of crazy ideas and activities, and I took part in everything. For the all-church talent show, I wrote a short melodrama straight from the silent film days, with many parts for volunteer actors. I even helped make pies for the ice cream social. None of it was my duty as a church member. I got involved because it distracted me from waiting and it was fun, though our projects made very little money. The most successful venture, dreamed up by a member who lived on a farm, required volunteers to prepare and sell lunches during livestock sales at the Monfort feed lot year round. Our club signed up for the winter schedule. Since there were no restaurants that far out in the country, we sold a ton of food.

On the morning I had signed up to work, fresh snow covered the ground, and the temperature registered in the bitter cold range. I drove to church to help prepare for the sale and told the crew I'd meet them at the auction barn after my class was over. I hurried back to campus, and in spite of bundling myself well for the weather, I shivered with cold. Once inside the heated basement classroom, warmth and a feeling of well-being wrapped me in a cheerful mood. I was eager to type and passed the first test without making a mistake.

Learning a new skill and being pregnant were both good things, and experiencing them at the same time felt magical. During the next hour I was on top of the world.

Before dismissing the class, the instructor reminded us to keep up the good work. I dreaded leaving the comfort of the cozy room and facing the outdoors again. Bracing myself for the frigid air, I left the building and hurried up the cement stairs. I noticed the coating of ice on the sidewalk just before I slipped on it, landing flat on my stomach. Slamming against the pavement knocked the wind out of me and sent my purse and notebook skidding in opposite directions. People rushed to help me up, and someone asked, "Are you all right?"

I couldn't breathe and gasped for air, shocked at how hard I'd hit the ground. I finally got my breath back, along with my purse and notebook, and heard someone ask again, "Are you all right?"

"Yes, I'm okay." *But is my baby okay?* A tingle of fear crawled up my spine.

I DROVE SLOWLY ON MY WAY BACK TO THE AUCTION BARN, PREOCCU-pied with worry about my fall. I pitched in to help sell food and tried to act normal by visiting and listening to the other women's chatter. Inside my head, a different conversation took place. I yearned to tell someone that I was pregnant and had just fallen on my stomach and was now worried sick. I have no idea why I didn't say what I was thinking. Instead, I watched their mouths move and smiled appro-priately while noticing how cold and shaky I felt. Then a slight hint of cramping stirred in my belly, followed by alarm bells in my head. The thought of what might be happening terrified me. The cramps grew stronger, and I knew I had to get home and lie down.

Because no one knew about my pregnancy, I excused myself by saying, "I'm so sorry, ladies, but I've gotta leave. I'm getting wicked stomach cramps." My brain was saying, *I hope they don't think I'm making this up to avoid working.*

One of the women winked and said, "So, Grandma's coming for a visit." Women understood that code, which meant your period had started.

I managed a weak smile and said, "Yeah, I guess so. She's early." Tears sat waiting behind my eyes, so I didn't linger. After I got in the car, I took several slow, deep breaths to calm myself before driving home.

BY THE TIME I GOT THERE, SOMETHING WARM HAD STARTED DRIBBLING down my legs. I knew it was blood before I reached the bathroom, where I sat on the toilet and cried. Grief stricken, I peeked into the toilet bowl and swear I saw a tiny shrimp. *Is that how babies look when they're getting started?*

I was so exhausted that my tears soon dried up, but I couldn't stop shivering. I heated water, filled the pink rubber hot water bottle, and crawled into bed. Slowly, my body relaxed, but my mind refused to stay quiet. I went over and over how I'd rushed up those steps, and I wished over and over that I'd taken more care and kept my eyes open for ice. I had never experienced such grief and longed for my husband to get home. I needed more than a hot water bottle to soothe my discomfort. I needed him.

A few hours later he came through the door, startled to see me in bed with eyes red and swollen from crying. He said, "Uh-oh ... what happened?"

I explained how I fell, and the flood of tears returned. My sadness rubbed off on him, and he lay beside me, held me close, and said, "We won't give up on starting our family. We'll try again." We stayed that way for a while before he said, "I'd better call Dr. Barber."

I heard Denny explain the details and then get quiet while listening to Dr. Barber's reply. He hung up and said, "Listen to this: the doctor thinks fertilization had probably attached very low in the uterus, and you could've lost it without ever falling down."

"Oh, no ... really?" A slight sense of relief trickled through me. *It might not be my fault.*

Then he said, "The doctor wants both of us to come in so he can see how you're doing and explain a different way of conceiving in the near future."

"A different way? Hon, we *know* how to make a baby."

"I guess it's a scientific method."

"Scientific sex? It sounds cold and unromantic."

"Let's just go and find out."

⁂

AT OUR APPOINTMENT, DR. BARBER EXAMINED ME AND SAID, "REST your body for a month before tying to conceive again. When you think you're pregnant, wait for three months without a period, and we'll run a test to confirm it."

Dr. Barber then launched into an explanation of conceiving the scientific way. The process determined the exact period of ovulation so a couple wouldn't waste energy or sperm. It involved Denny keeping a chart to record my temperature every single morning before I used the bathroom or moved at all.

I found it hard to follow, but he was all ears while learning about the Basal Body Temperature system of birth control (BBT for short). If not for my husband's complete understanding, I would've been calling Dr. Barber repeatedly for further directions. But first, I had to rest for a month. That was a long time to wait. When a woman wants to conceive, she wants it to happen immediately.

My husband found a book at the library that explained BBT in detail. We read it together. After the first chapter, I felt a shift in my attitude and began to embrace the words, thinking, *This is kind of interesting.* Learning a scientific way to conceive gave me a lift.

The BBT method required diligence. Each morning, Denny would have to place a thermometer under my tongue, hold it for two minutes, and jot down the reading. He said, "Ya know what? I really appreciate the controlled aspect of this system. By keeping a daily log, we'll know *exactly* when ovulation happens." Then his eyes widened, and he added, "I'll make a graph." I'd never seen my husband so eager to make a chart.

THE MONTH OF RESTING EVENTUALLY PASSED, AND WE WERE READY TO trust science. A thermometer, pencil, and chart waited in my husband's nightstand. As soon as his alarm went off the next day, he tapped my forehead.

"Betty, wake up. I hafta take your temperature."

"What?"

"Your temperature?"

"Oh, yeah. I hafta go to the toilet first."

"You're not supposed to move ... or talk. Just open your mouth. Don't bite down."

"Okay."

I held the thing under my tongue for two whole minutes while he watched the clock. When he said, "Ninety-seven point five," he sounded like an announcer at the Olympics. He marked it on the graph as if it were the most important job in the world. I felt a rush of affection for his commitment. I went to the bathroom before jumping back under the covers, while he ate breakfast and left for school.

For the first week, my temperature hovered near 97.5. That straight, flat line across the graph bored me. I was eager to ovulate as soon as possible. One Sunday, the number rose to 97.7, and our eyes brightened. On Monday it held, rising a bit more on Tuesday. By Wednesday, it reached 97.9 and stayed there on Thursday. Watching him enter a number on the graph every morning had taken on an air of excitement; it became a weird kind of foreplay. When the thermometer read 98.0 on Friday and held for twenty-four hours, we looked at each other, awestruck. With wonder and astonishment in his voice, Denny said, "Tonight's the night."

An hour later, my mother called. "Hi, Betty. I'm in Greeley visiting friends. Is it okay if I stay at your place tonight?"

Egads! I wanted to say, "No, Mom. We're making a baby tonight." Instead, I said, "Sure ... that would be nice."

When Den came home for lunch, I told him about the call. He said, "We'll put your mother in our bedroom. You can sleep on the couch in the living room, and I'll sleep on the floor. When she starts snoring as loud as she always does, you can join me on the floor, and we'll get the job done." He made it sound like a class assignment.

I FELT TENSE AND WORRIED ALL EVENING. SOON AFTER MOM WENT TO bed, her snoring vibrated through the wall, assuring us she wouldn't hear a thing. He got right to work with the first step by placing two sofa pillows under my hips to raise them as described in the book. I nearly fell off the pile. When he tossed one aside, it hit a chair. I held my breath, worried that the noise would wake Mom. I was a nervous wreck. I said, "Honey, forget foreplay. Just do your thing," and he did.

He broke the speed record for insemination so we could concentrate on the second step: keeping my hips raised for ten minutes so no baby makers could escape. I dozed off in that position. When I awoke with blood rushing to my head, I turned onto my side and saw him fast asleep on the couch, where I was supposed to be. I pushed the pillows away, curled under the blankets, and imagined how sperm introduced itself to egg. Was it a slow, seductive process, or did sperm just throw himself headlong against egg, causing her to say, "Slow down. What's the hurry? We got all night."? We didn't know it yet, but when the Denny sperm met the Betty egg, they bonded and started going steady.

THREE MONTHS PASSED WITH NO PERIOD, SO I MADE AN APPOINTMENT for the test with a female frog from Africa. Dr. Barber injected my urine into the frog's dorsal lymph sac, and twelve hours later, she laid eggs.

Oh joyful, joyful! I was once again with child.

My carefree happiness didn't last long. The next month, an evil spell seemed to fall upon me, because I felt sick every morning. I hadn't prepared myself for that, and it was awful. I couldn't think about eggs—boiled, scrambled, or fried—without retching. I craved lemon slices with salt. Denny called it the pregnant woman's version of a margarita. I thought it was funny, but Dr. Barber said, "I don't think daily lemon consumption is good for the enamel on your teeth." I couldn't give it up, so I rinsed my mouth after each lemon fix. I also craved radishes and the crunch of ice cubes. My taste bud sensitivity was so amplified that it made evening meals in the girls' dining hall a divine experience. I had second helpings every night without guilt. But second helpings came with a price.

I gained so much weight that Dr. Barber said, "Don't take seconds." I did as he told me but still gained weight. Even with smaller servings, the hearty nature of the evening meals meant for college kids proved too rich for me. I had the glow that pregnancy brings on, but beneath the glow toddled a blimp filled with water. With every step, I sloshed. I was so encumbered that it was hard to walk straight, and I swayed from side to side. With a child growing inside me, I ballooned from 120 pounds to 160. I was pretty sure water retention was more to blame for my increasing weight than overeating, because my face, hands, and feet swelled, too.

One evening I said, "Den, it's time to go eat."

When I sighed, he stopped reading the paper and asked with sympathy, "Do you want me to carry you to the dining hall?"

My feet hurt so bad that I said, "Yeah, I'd really like that."

CHAPTER 23

Waiting and Planning

W E DREADED THE THOUGHT OF MOVING AGAIN, BUT DENNY'S one-year fellowship was about to expire. Though we had no idea where we'd go next, we had to go somewhere. Hand in hand, we headed to the placement office together, prepared for a long wait before finding a teaching position west of the Mississippi. My husband was good at everything. If they asked him to teach ants how to swim, he could do it.

The employment counselor said, "So we're looking for a job teaching math, right?"

"That's right."

"Let's see what we've got here. If nothing is available, we'll put your application on file."

Filled with a sense of expectation, we sat ramrod straight while the fellow thumbed through his files. He grabbed a card and said, "Mr. Auchard, how's this? Math teacher. Cheyenne, Wyoming."

"Not bad; let's remember that one."

"Okay. Here's something in Albuquerque."

"Maybe. Let's take a look at a few more."

"How about junior high math in Emporia, Kansas?"

The word *Kansas* got our attention. The counselor noticed our interest and handed us the description so we could learn the details. It was similar to what Den had been doing in Greeley. The location was the campus secondary school, where they trained teachers, and

Emporia State College had a good reputation. As a bonus, we'd be close to his family.

My excitement level soared, and I said, "Honey, Kansas is not that far away. Let's start packing our stuff this weekend and move as soon as the baby is born."

"Good idea. But I should probably apply for the position first."

The counselor raised his eyebrows. "Oh, you're having a baby?" We nodded in unison, and he inquired about the due date.

My husband answered for both of us. "August 27th."

"Wow. You're planning to give birth and move right after it's born?"

We looked at each other with pride and said, "Yeah."

We had no idea that a new mother was usually whacked after going through labor and delivery. Neither of us realized the amount of energy required to care for a newborn or how scary it could be. I'd been concentrating on getting ready for natural child*birth* instead of preparing myself for child*care*.

The counselor gave us a copy of the information for the Emporia State position. As soon as we got back to the dorm, Den placed a call to make sure it was still available. The head of the teacher education department was so eager to hire someone that he asked to hear his resume over the phone. Dr. Rollo occasionally interrupted to ask a question. At the end of the conversation, he said, "You're hired. The paperwork will go out today."

The relief of finding a job so fast was cause for celebration. We ate hamburgers at a diner and then saw the movie *Singin' in the Rain.*

WITH THE JOB SEARCH BEHIND US, I RETURNED TO LEARNING MORE about delivering a baby the natural way. The book that enthralled me that summer was one Denny had picked up in the college library. Dr. Grantly Dick-Read, the British author of *Childbirth without Fear*, wrote that fear leads to muscle tension, which causes most of the pain women experience during labor. He believed that breathing exercises and relaxation techniques could help mothers give birth with less discomfort. This sounded like up-to-date thinking, so I decided to use his methods to prepare myself.

I was so determined to deliver by the natural method that I studied his book as if it were the most important thing in my life. I should have been reading articles about how to sterilize bottles and formula. I already knew I wouldn't be breast feeding. Dr. Barber had told me my nipples were inverted, which would prevent an infant from latching on. Two years later, l proved him wrong.

I envisioned the process of giving birth as being as simple as making a grocery list and buying what was on it. In my head, it went something like this:

1. Go to the hospital on the due date.
2. Have the baby.
3. Stay in the hospital for a few days to rest and get acquainted with our new son or daughter.
4. Help load the car with our belongings.
5. Wake the little one, give it a bottle, and change its diaper.
6. Get in the car and drive to Kansas to our new apartment.

My imaginary plan was as practical as leaving two puppies alone for a weekend, but we learned everything the hard way, by making lots of mistakes.

⚜

CHAPTER 24

Waiting and Creating

WHILE A NEW LIFE GREW IN MY BELLY, I GREW IN EXPERIENCE and maturity. I was still housemother to thirty-six girls who needed no guidance from us. They were all fairly independent young women.

We ate dinner with them every night. As my pregnancy progressed, we got into the habit of leaving Gordon Hall before the girls to give me plenty of time to waddle to the dining room. With my extra pounds, walking required such effort that I always felt out of breath upon arrival.

We enjoyed sitting at a different table each evening so we could get acquainted with more students. Rongratana Isarabakni, a thirty-two-year-old woman from Thailand, captured my attention.

Rongrat was living in Snyder Hall until she could find an apartment close to campus. A pleasant, inquisitive woman with a gentle but formal manner, she was working on a doctorate in education. She refused to call us by our first names, explaining that it wouldn't be respectful. She said, "Mr. Auchard is a teacher here, and both of you are responsible for many young women. I think of you as our leaders."

"But what if we gave you permission to call us Denny and Betty?"

"Oh, no. I have not earned the privilege, but perhaps someday."

I was truly disappointed, hoping to be friends rather than acquaintances.

In spite of her formality and respect for custom, Rongrat often surprised us with an out-of-the blue comment. One night she said, "Mrs. Auchard, your baby will be quite large, yes?"

157

"Do you really think so?"

"Yes, but your large belly might also mean twins."

That had never occurred to me. Although I hadn't given any thought to the details of caring for an infant, I was horrified at the possibility of taking care of two at once. My husband looked at me out of the corner of his eyes and grinned. Then Rongrat turned to him and said, "Mr. Auchard. You are Eee-tal-lee-an, yes?"

"No, my mother is Irish, and my father is French. Why do you ask?"

"You are veddy dark and quite handsome."

Denny blushed and said nothing.

He *was* dark and handsome, especially in the summer. And with his black hair, he could've passed for Mediterranean.

Rongrat adorned herself with unique jewelry, and I looked forward to whatever ornament she might wear next. When she wore a silver lapel pin, it caught my eye. The female Balinese dancer had been crafted in a traditional pose, with knees, elbows, and wrists bent at right angles. Rongrat allowed me to borrow her pin overnight to make a drawing, and she also loaned me several magazines from Thailand. Every page revealed dazzling pictures of dancers, and I went slowly so I could savor each image. The costumes and makeup were stunning. The dancers arranged their limbs into positions that seemed impossible. They were artful contortionists. I made endless sketches, because I'd had a fascination with Balinese art forms since high school after seeing them in movies.

In my senior year, I sweet-talked my girlfriend into performing a Balinese dance with me for school assembly. She said, "I don't know anything about that stuff."

I said, "We'll invent it. The kids won't know the difference, and it'll be a kick."

We bought a tube of Brylcreem and slicked our hair flat against our heads so it appeared to be painted onto our skulls. The ad said, "Just a little dab'll do ya," but we needed more than a dab and used most of the tube. Then we sprinkled sparkles on top of our slicked-down hair, and they stuck as if the Brylcreem were glue. Then we used lipstick, rouge, and eyebrow pencil to turn our faces into stylized masks. Wearing our pajamas and lots of bracelets around our ankles, we performed barefoot. Keeping our shoulders immobile, we slid our necks from side to side the way they did in the movies.

The 45 rpm record we found was the perfect music for our routine, with twangy stringed instruments, tinkling bells, and clunking wooden sticks that contributed to the odd rhythm. The dance moves we invented were unlike anything we'd ever seen in an assembly. Although the performance was meant to be serious, the audience laughed. Did we care? No, because they gave us a standing ovation and cheered until we repeated our little show.

RECALLING THE EVENT ALWAYS WARMED MY HEART, BECAUSE I'D LOVED performing in plays and crazy skits at school. But I was about to become a mother and had no time to indulge in treasured teenage memories, even if they did make me smile. Still, I studied Rongrat's magazines as if they were Pulitzer prize winners and used my drawings from the Thai magazines for a copper tooling class I'd joined. The craft shop owner offered patterns for sale, but I said, "Oh, I've created two of my own."

He looked at them and said, "These will be too hard if you've never done tooling."

I said, "Well, I'd like to try."

He said, "Okay ...," with a tone that I interpreted as a warning.

Tooling *was* hard, because you worked on the front and back of the copper sheet to create a bas-relief image. I spent hours on my project, which caused my hands to ache. I finished the female dancer first and antiqued the copper with liver of sulfur. Then I polished the surface with fine steel wool and painted the background a bright teal lacquer. I worked on my male and female dancers every day for two weeks.

Denny finished them with a burlap border and teal-colored frame. I was so proud that I showed Rongrat. She said, "Mrs. Auchard, you are an artist." After all that hard work, I truly believed her.

I shared my accomplishment with friends at church, and one woman said, "Betty, I hope you keep up your artwork after you become a mother."

"Of *course* I will." I actually believed that.

Two couples at church wanted a set of Balinese dancers just like mine. I told them I couldn't duplicate the patterns, because they were so complex that a copy would never look the same. Instead, I suggested they pick designs from my other drawings. Three church members soon owned copper-tooled dancers, each of them an original, with nothing duplicated.

I charged fifteen dollars for a pair. Although the price was low, I still felt I was charging too much. I wasn't trying to make money. I labored over them because I loved what I was doing. It also got my mind off the discomfort of my ankles, which had become fat, and my body, which had turned puffy.

Den caught my creative fever and spent a weekend making an enlarger, using a lens he'd rescued from the big fire at York College. Our coat closet became a darkroom. He made exposures with an old box camera, developed the film, and printed the pictures. Maybe all the creativity we were experiencing would rub off on our child the way my mother thought it could.

⁕

WHEN MOM WAS PREGNANT WITH ME, SHE WANTED HER CHILD TO BE as creative and innovative as her family. She believed that if she thought good thoughts and listened only to classical music, it would happen. And, I *did* follow in their footsteps. I wasn't convinced that my interests would rub off on the tiny person growing in my body. But just in case, I often turned the radio to the classical music station.

Balinese Dancers

Years later, when our son David was seven, he asked his dad to check out classical albums at the library so he could pretend to be the conductor. He was *always* conducting, so it must have worked.

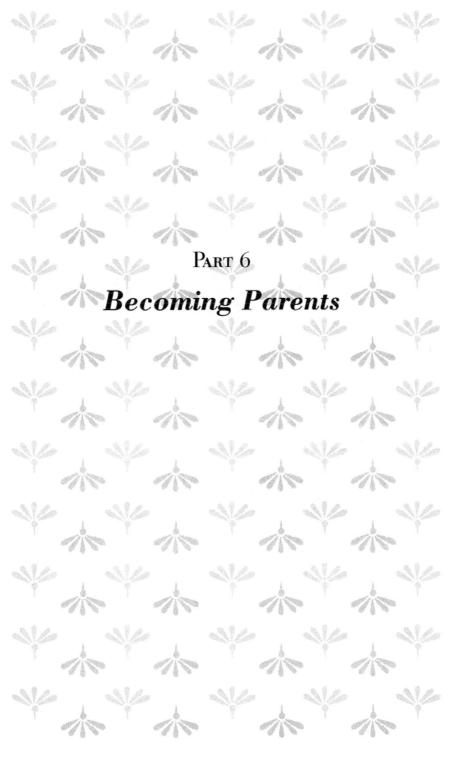

PART 6

Becoming Parents

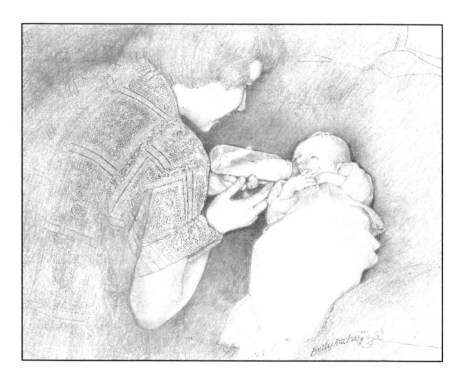

Betty Feeds Baby Dave

CHAPTER 25

Hello, Baby

O N MY TWENTY-SECOND BIRTHDAY, A WEEK FROM MY DUE DATE, THE girls in the dorm gave us a surprise baby shower. Ever since getting caught with dirty hair and wearing a raggedy housecoat, I'd never cared much for surprise parties. This time I was clean and dressed in acceptable attire.

Den and I took turns tearing gift wrap from a mountain of presents. After we opened the last package, which revealed a music box, I started thanking the girls. One of them said, "Mrs. A, here's something else," and handed me an envelope with a gift certificate for diaper service. It had a strange effect on me.

Diaper service didn't have the same ring as *cutie patootie booties*. Diaper service meant business. It sounded down and dirty, and that's when the reality of imminent motherhood hit me. I was lost in thought when someone returned me to the present by asking, "Mr. A, what're you going to call the baby?"

He said, "We're keen about two names, so if it's a girl, we'll name her Rhoda Denise."

Then I jumped in. "If it's a boy, we'll name him David Lester after Denny's youngest brother."

A FEW DAYS AFTER THE SHOWER, SEMESTER BREAK ARRIVED, AND most people on campus left for home or someplace where they could party for a week. We were alone until five family members from out of state arrived for the birth of our first child. My husband's parents, brother, sister-in-law, and niece stayed in a hotel at night and socialized with us during the day. Since no one else used the dormitory kitchen or reception area during the break, we claimed them as though we owned the place.

We enjoyed our time together and did a lot of eating, chatting, and telling family stories while waiting for the main event to begin. But the star of the show must've had stage fright, because he failed to appear. August 27 came and went, and the relatives couldn't stay any longer. They returned to Kansas, saying, "Call us as soon as you become parents."

My parents had separated again and hadn't been in touch. They knew of my pregnancy but probably forgot the due date. I didn't mind. I'd become accustomed to their inconsistent lifestyle, which included not staying in touch.

THE NEXT DAY, DR. BARBER CALLED TO SEE HOW I WAS DOING. IN HIS opinion, my delivery was overdue, so he admitted me to the hospital for a series of seven injections. I didn't realize it was Labor Day until the nurse pointed it out.

The doctor said, "The action usually gets going after the first two injections."

Denny and I beamed with anticipation. We would soon meet our child.

The nurse came in and said, "Okay, Mrs. Auchard. Let's get started. Are you ready?"

Was I ready? Yes ... absolutely, positively ready.

Although I'd prepared myself for a needle prick, it seemed like nothing happened, a great way to start.

She removed the syringe and said, "In about thirty minutes you might notice slight cramping. If not, we'll administer the second shot, and that usually gets things rolling."

Den sat by the bed, holding my hand and rubbing my arm. Ordinarily, his concern would've been welcome. Instead, it made me nervous. I tried to relax and pretend that having him rub my arm soothed me. After twenty minutes, he asked, "Do you feel anything yet?"

Nothing unusual had happened, so I shook my head in response. Maybe I'd been breathing wrong or holding my legs in the wrong position. Perhaps I'd pinched a nerve without knowing it. The nurse returned, found a new spot to poke, and injected me again.

Then Denny asked, "Are you nervous?" I couldn't decide how I felt and shrugged my shoulders, hoping it didn't appear that I had shrugged off his question. We stopped talking after that. I feared conversation might interfere with the medication and paid attention to every little twinge, willing it to turn into something dramatic. Then I remembered all the reading I'd done about natural childbirth. Hey, that was it. I had prepared so well, I wouldn't have any pain, and my infant would just slide out when it was supposed to.

When nothing happened after the fifth injection, I became worried and asked, "Do you suppose something's wrong with the baby?"

The nurse said, "Oh, no. We can tell the baby's fine. It's probably not ready to come out, but we'll give you the last two injections anyway. If nothing happens after that, the only thing you can do is go back home and wait. This medication doesn't work for everyone."

What a disappointment. I'd assumed those shots were a sure thing, but they sure weren't working for me. Maybe my lack of pain wasn't the result of preparing for natural childbirth after all. I remembered something old-timers used to say about the modern practice of inducing labor: "When the apple's ripe, it'll fall."

We dragged our weary selves back to the dorm and let the days pass, hardly knowing what to do. Waiting around for something to happen used up all my energy. Three days later, we'd gotten caught up in a radio program after dinner when a barely detectable twinge captured my attention. I said, "Honey, something just happened."

He turned the radio off in very slow motion, as though any fast movement might scare it away, and whispered, "Do you still feel it?"

I whispered back, "It's gone."

We waited. Five minutes later, I put both hands on my stomach and nodded. He knew what I meant.

The sensation was so delicate I assumed I *had* done a good job of preparing myself after all. We decided to keep track of the barely noticeable pangs. They never changed in intensity but became more frequent. We called the advice nurse, and she said to come on in.

The admitting nurse recognized us and said, "I see that you're joining us again."

"Yes, I think I'm having contractions about two and one-half minutes apart."

"You *think* you're having contractions?"

"Yes, but they're so soft it's hard to time them."

"Are you having one now?"

"No. It just fluttered away."

She left to talk to her supervisor. During her absence, the next fluttering in my belly seemed a tiny bit stronger, so I was relieved when she returned and said, "My supervisor says to get you admitted and into a room."

My relief turned to concern when I discovered that my roommate was having more than flutters. She wailed so loud and long that I wondered if she'd been hit by a semi truck. Her poor husband sat nearby, appearing helpless. While observing them, I couldn't tell what I was feeling. If they were contractions, mine were nothing compared to my roommate's. When she started screaming, her husband almost fainted, and I clenched my fists. Things changed in a hurry when the woman almost delivered in her bed. Nurses put her on a gurney so fast I never had a chance to introduce myself. In nothing flat, they brought in someone else, who screamed as loudly as the patient who had just left. By then, I was scared stiff.

Over the next sixty minutes, my mild sense of tightening turned into a hard stomach that never softened. Dr. Barber paid me a visit to oversee the event. He placed his hand on my belly and said, "I feel this contraction. Let's see how long it lasts."

"Dr. Barber, it never goes away. It's been this way for an hour. I have no pain, though my back aches a little."

He turned to the nurse. "Let's put Betty in a private room. This commotion is scaring away her labor."

She looked at her eyebrows as if thinking, *Oh, please*, but transferred me anyway. After I spent an hour in the private room with no progress, Dr. Barber said, "We're going to move you into delivery and find out what's going on here."

They hoisted me onto a gurney and wheeled me into a cold delivery room, where I shivered under a warm blanket. After I sucked happy gas into my lungs, nothing mattered. My thoughts drifted, and I carried on a conversation with anyone who came near me.

In my dreamy state, I imagined that many nurses and doctors gathered around me because my case was so unusual. I heard comments such as *no pain, aching back, hard stomach, what to do?* It sounded as though they were talking through toilet paper tubes, and I wondered what it all meant. I heard worry in Dr. Barber's voice when he said, "We'll have to take out her liver."

Take out my liver? Why?

I don't remember what happened after that.

⁂

DAVID LESTER AUCHARD CAME INTO THE WORLD ON SEPTEMBER 4, 1952, without my knowing it. After I sobered up, a nurse brought him to me so I could finally hold him. He was 21 inches long and weighed 8½ pounds. What a sturdy boy. But the shape of his head scared me. I couldn't stop caressing it to coax the point down. Dr. Barber noticed and offered some assurance. "It won't stay that way. It'll return to a round shape in a couple of weeks."

"Why is it like that?"

"His head is pointed because he came out in a posterior position, which means face down. Babies are usually born face up. He got stuck in the birth canal for so long it changed the shape of his skull. But don't worry. An infant's skull is in four overlapping pieces so it can change shape to accommodate the birthing process."

The cartoon character Denny Dimwit came to mind. He'd worn a dunce cap in school so often that by the time he removed it, his head had become as pointed as the cap.

When my eyes drifted to David's red temples, Dr. Barber explained that, too. "He was so stuck that we had to use forceps to grab him. You can see where some of the skin is scraped off."

Of course I could see it. My poor child looked like he'd been beaten up while being born.

Then Dr. Barber said, "Betty, your tailbone will be painful for a while. During the delivery, the baby almost broke it. I'll tell Denny to put a board under your mattress."

He also reminded me to continue taking the pills for drying up my milk, because I wouldn't be able to breast feed with inverted nipples. Even though I had accepted that fact before my son's birth, after holding him, I wanted to breast feed my baby more than anything in the world. Nature was cruel.

Then, out of nowhere, Dr. Barber chuckled and said, "By the way, Betty, about your liver ..."

"My liver? Oh, yeah. Why did you remove it?"

"I didn't. You were dreaming during the delivery."

The old brown brick hospital in Greeley had no private toilets in the patient rooms. Aides helped new mothers walk down the hall when we had to "go." I could barely move my feet even with her holding my arm. I was convinced that my baby-birthing parts were ripping open. To keep my insides from falling out, I clutched my crotch as I shuffled down the hall. The aide asked, "What's wrong, Mrs. Auchard? Are you going to pee before we reach the toilet?"

"No, I'm holding my guts in place."

⁂

I TOLD DR. BARBER ABOUT OUR UPCOMING MOVE TO ANOTHER STATE and that I wanted to leave the hospital as soon as possible. He said, "That's fine as long as you have help at home."

"Oh, yes, I'll have plenty of help." I'd have my husband, and I was sure he would be enough.

The doctor gave me a pill to get my bowels to move and then released me a day and a half after delivery. Only after getting home did I realize the frightful condition of my body. Episiotomy stitches covered so much territory I was sure my nether regions were made of wood. I could hardly walk and began to question whether we'd be able to handle the pressure of moving so soon.

The hospital sent two bottles of formula with us, along with the recipe for making more. I assumed two bottles would last all day, but David wanted both of them immediately. I guess he'd worked up an appetite on the ride from the hospital to our apartment. We hadn't yet purchased the paraphernalia to make formula. Why? I don't remember. We were naïve.

Our little son cried very hard, and Denny said, "I'll dash to the store to get what we need to feed him. What is it we need?"

With recipe in hand, I said, "Write this down: canned milk, corn syrup, baby bottles, and a canning kettle with a rack inside."

"Okay, you rock him while I shop."

"Hon, we don't have a rocker."

"I mean just hold him against your chest and rock back and forth."

I did what he suggested to calm David down, but it hurt my stitches to rock on them, so I just moved my arms. We'd been home for less than an hour, and I was already worn out.

⁂

It seemed Den was gone forever. I kept my arms moving in a rocking motion, but David cried harder. My husband finally returned from the store and washed, rinsed, and dried the new equipment in such a meticulous manner one might've thought our kitchen was a laboratory. Only then did he start measuring the ingredients for the formula. David continued screaming while my husband, the perfectionist, spent more than an hour mixing the concoction, pouring it into bottles, and sterilizing the whole lot.

In those days, parents sterilized anything that touched the precious lips of an infant. If I'd known then what I know now, I would've dumped the ingredients together with warm water from the faucet, sloshed it into the bottle, and fed our screaming child.

In my state of body and mind, the process seemed to go on for a hundred years. Without a doubt, real life had hit us smack dab in the forehead. My husband was abnormally painstaking with every step because he was as nervous as I was.

While he watched the clock, my laxative kicked in. I had to get to the bathroom fast. I put David in his laundry-basket bassinet and inched my way to the toilet. To my horror, I didn't make it in time and had an accident on the floor. Then I slipped in the muck and fell down hard. My stitches were already hurting, and they hurt a lot worse after that. I was pretty sure I'd injured something inside my body.

David's screaming kept Denny from hearing me hit the floor. I wanted to lie there in the mess I'd made and cry and yell for help, but I couldn't. Yelling for help meant Den would stop what he was doing. I forced myself to clean up the floor first and my body next. It took a while, because the struggle of getting up and down made the bad situation worse.

By the time I'd finished in the bathroom, changed my clothes, and eased myself into the kitchen, the formula had cooled off enough to feed David. He guzzled it down and conked out immediately.

THE FIRST FEW HOURS ON OUR OWN WERE A NIGHTMARE I WOULD never forget. It was as though a tornado had tossed us about and left us in shambles. We remained tense and scared as we struggled to take charge. When talking about those events years later, my husband would say, "I was fine and not a bit worried." I knew better.

We were both anxious about everything after becoming parents, especially the unnerving practice of circumcision. It seemed necessary, and nobody questioned it, but circumcision horrified me. We'd wounded our son on purpose, leaving him with an injured penis in addition to a pointed head and raw temples. On top of all that, his umbilical cord stuck out like a dried twig, and the doctor warned us not to break it off, saying, "It'll drop off when it's ready." Gruesome imagery ripped through my mind at the horror of knocking the "twig" off prematurely. I feared it would leave a hole, and the baby's intestines might leak out.

Anxiety kept me a hair's breadth away from panic. Denny tried not to show his concern and kept moving and taking care of things. I had my birth injuries, and our son had his, and the new dad did his best to take care of both of us.

When I reflect on how my dreamy image of a new baby clashed with fact, I don't know whether to laugh or be ashamed. We were simply unprepared. That might be why my husband's version of the events and mine differed. He was too embarrassed to tell the truth.

CHAPTER 26

Mom to the Rescue

A S ANXIOUS FIRST-TIME PARENTS, WE HANDLED OUR BABY WITH such caution it seemed we were afraid of him. What we were afraid of was the possibility of hurting one of his three trouble spots. After changing his diaper, we often sat side by side while I fed our infant son, both of us staring at his precious face as he fell asleep in my arms. I should have napped, too, because I was dog tired, but I couldn't bear to put him down. I would hold him and study his features until my arms ached.

No matter how much we wanted to sit and admire our first child, we had to cut it short. Boxes and belongings cluttered both rooms, and we needed to organize the mess before driving to Kansas the next week. Denny's job was to sort through everything and decide what would go in the car with us and what would be shipped to his parents' home. They had agreed to store our belongings until we found a rental in Emporia.

Before leaving, we would have time to get used to taking care of our baby and then rest up for a few days. That was our plan ... until the phone rang. It was for Den. By the time he hung up, he appeared very solemn and said, "I can't believe this. The school administration wants me there a week early to attend faculty meetings and workshops."

"What? A week early? That means we'd have to leave here in three days."

"That's right."

"We can't possibly do that. Call and tell them it's too soon for us to travel."

Denny said, "I've gotta think this through. It's a new job, and I can't afford to start off by turning down a request."

"They should've told you earlier instead of at the last minute. I'm sure they'll understand that we can't travel yet."

"I can make arrangements for someone to stay here with you and the baby for a few days while I go on ahead. Then I'll arrange for both of you to fly to Kansas the following week."

Panic raged through me like a flooded river. The calm I'd felt only five minutes earlier suddenly turned into resentment and fear. It was not a good feeling. I had to find a way to accept that my husband felt obligated to attend the mandatory meetings.

I couldn't believe the unwelcome turn of events. I had no idea what to do. I was too agitated to come up with a plan, so I decided to let Den do the planning.

Supervisors for each dorm were still on campus preparing to greet incoming freshmen in the fall. Denny paid a visit to the woman in charge of Snyder Hall, Mrs. Blackwell. He told her why I shouldn't travel and asked if David and I could stay in an empty dormitory room near her apartment. She agreed. He also asked if she would feed me and look in on us after he left. She agreed to that, as well, and he paid her thirty dollars ahead of time. She turned down the money. When he insisted, she said, "Well ... okay."

BEFORE WE RELOCATED TO SNYDER HALL, DENNY TOOK CHARGE OF almost everything. My painful stitches and injured tailbone created a lack of coordination, so I couldn't do much on my own. He changed our son's diapers, packed the car with more boxes, and taught me how to make infant formula. Standing for long periods wore me out, so I bypassed his meticulous method for preparing it. Fortunately, he was too busy packing to notice.

Giving birth and relocating a week later had been a flight of the imagination that sounded easy before it happened. The reality wasn't at all easy. I finally understood why the job counselor had been so wide-eyed with disbelief when we announced with such casualness, "Yes, we're moving right after our baby is born." We had no idea how crazy that sounded, but *he* knew.

My husband had his work cut out for him, emptying our apartment and shipping boxes to Kansas. That done, he got us settled in the other dorm so we could practice our routine with Mrs. Blackwell. He stayed with us for two days. We each had a twin bed, and the laundry-basket bassinet sat on a desk next to the window. Dormitory rooms came with a sink but no toilet. During my freshmen year, I'd lived on the second floor of the same building. At that time, the community bathroom at the end of the hall had not been a problem. Now it seemed a mile away.

I dreaded Denny leaving more than I could possibly tell him, but I kept it to myself. Otherwise, both of us would've been frantic. The truth was that I felt afraid to be on my own while taking care of an infant's needs along with mine. Everything in my body hurt, but the worst pain was in my heart. As the day for him to leave grew closer, both of us became apprehensive. I sensed that he was worried about how I would cope, but his concern about offending his employers was greater than his fear of leaving us behind. I forced myself to put on a brave front the day he left. Like it or not, I had to deal with the situation.

Denny later confessed that when he was barely outside of town, he pulled over to sop up his tears and pull himself together. I'm glad I never saw that. I would've fallen apart.

❧

With my husband gone, no matter how careful I tried to be, I moved around too much doing tasks on my own. It caused my body to hurt even more. Mrs. Blackwell helped with small jobs when she could, but she was preoccupied with preparations for incoming freshmen who would arrive soon. On my first day alone, she mixed formula while I kept David clean and dry, put salve on his temples and circumcision, and gently caressed his pointed head to make it rounder. She showed me the cupboard where she kept breakfast supplies, making it possible for me to do that on my own. At noon and dinner time she knocked on my door, and we ate together in her apartment kitchen. My room was across the hall, which made it easy to hear the baby cry if he needed attention.

The arrangement was convenient and doable. But in the middle of our first night alone, David woke up fretful. I warmed a bottle and tried to feed him. He wouldn't take it. I wondered if it could be colic, something I'd read about. Caring for a fussy infant scared me, because I didn't know how to help him. I rubbed his tummy. No luck. Finally, I picked him up and paced. I changed his diaper and returned to pacing and patting. Nothing worked, and my back was killing me. I was so weak I felt faint.

Fear and exhaustion caused me to cry, and I started a walking prayer, repeating over and over, "God, please don't let me faint. Please don't let me faint. I'll fall and hurt the baby. God, please don't let me faint." The idea of falling while holding David terrified me, and praying gave me strength to keep moving. Before I had a chance to fall apart completely, he fell asleep, because he had worn himself out. *Thank you, God; thank you, God.* I lowered my son into the bassinette with great care for fear of waking him.

By then, I was certain that if I didn't lie down, I'd fall down. I couldn't climb into bed the normal way with an injured tailbone; instead, I had to lean against the wall and lower myself onto the bed, shifting to avoid pressing on any tender places. I talked to my body in soothing tones, persuading my chest to relax. Then I charmed my arms into letting go, and sweet-talked my legs into going limp. Finally, I gave my feet permission to take a break. I wasn't aware of merging with the mattress but didn't wake until three hours later. David was still asleep.

I needed to use the toilet. Getting out of bed meant clawing my way up the wall for support and letting my legs drop over the edge of the mattress until my feet touched the floor. Once upright, I still had to shuffle down a long hallway. I stood there for a few minutes and said to the empty air, "I can't take care of both of us." I forced my body to move while desperate thoughts raced through my mind: *I need more help than Mrs. Blackwell can give. What shall I do? Who can I call? Is there anyone at church who would stay with me? But I can't throw myself on the mercy of others. If I have to explain how desperate I am, I'll start crying and not know how to stop.*

During the grueling walk back to my room, I noticed the pay phone on the wall and remembered that each dorm had one on every floor. I decided to send a telegram to my mother. I needed family. I retrieved my coin purse, emptied loose change into my palm, and inched my way back down the hall to the phone. First I asked the operator how much a telegram would cost. Money and message had to come out even. I counted the coins and, thank God, had enough for one line, which I dictated: *Mom, Denny had to leave for his job. We have a boy. I need your help. Betty.*

When I said the words "I need your help," the operator must have sensed that I was close to tears. She said, "Take a deep breath, dear. There's no rush."

I dropped all the coins into the slots and came up ten cents short. She said, "Don't worry, dear. I'll punch it up on this end."

With a tight throat, my "thank you" came out as a squeak. I'd become an emotional mess, and I couldn't do anything about it.

She said, "I'm sending this to your mama right now, so everything's gonna be fine."

I knew she was looking after me. I hung up and cried all the way to the room to lie down until my son needed attention again.

THAT EVENING, WHILE THE BABY NAPPED, I NEEDED TO GO TO THE toilet and didn't dare wait, because making it down the hall took a long time. I sat in a stall with the door wide open to hear him if he cried. My body and spirit had become so unstable that I buried my face in my hands and prayed, "God, let Mom answer the telegram; please tell her to come to my rescue." I was rocking from side to side, because the movement comforted me, when I heard, "Betty?"

Mrs. Blackwell probably wondered where I was. She called my name again and asked, "Betty, where are you?"

That's not Mrs. Blackwell.

I called out, "Mom, I'm in the bathroom!"

"Where's the bathroom?"

"Just keep walking down the hall toward my voice."

She ambled in with a hand on each hip and asked, "What the hell happened? Your dad said you sent a telegram asking for my help because Denny left you after the baby was born."

I laughed and cried at the same time. Oh, how it hurt. But what a miracle that Mom arrived just as I was praying for her to rescue me. I didn't know who or what God might be, but I sure prayed a lot after our son was born. Once Mom heard the whole story of why I needed her, we settled into the dorm like roommates, with a newborn to nurture. My mother fed David Lester Auchard, her first grandchild, and changed his diapers.

I flopped on the bed and allowed myself to fall apart, and it felt wonderful. I told Mom not to worry, because it was time to get rid of the extra tears I'd held onto for two days. Crying for a while released some of the tension and exhaustion. While I whimpered, she studied her grandson's face and tried not to look concerned about his pointed head, which I would have to explain later.

Finally, I could relax, thankful that my mother had arrived to take care of me, too.

Betty, Denny, and David

CHAPTER 27

Another Mother to the Rescue

MOM AND I BECAME ADVERSARIES WHEN I TURNED THIRTEEN. Though we seemed to get along for a spell, we'd always clash again. I loved her but didn't like her very much. However, the older we got, the more tolerant we both became. Having her show up after David's birth was a miracle that turned me into an appreciative daughter. Perhaps having a child of my own helped me understand her better.

Mom and I talked about motherhood during David's naps, and she told stories about the family and friends who helped her after she delivered me. Because I weighed ten pounds at birth, she needed all kinds of assistance. Our conversation was going so well that I felt comfortable asking if she and Dad would get together again.

She said, "Probably. I guess we need some distance from each other now and then."

Apparently nothing had changed. They were still bouncing apart and back together as they had done all of my life. Maybe it was the only way they could make their relationship work.

After Mom arrived, she took over fixing the baby's formula and got permission to do some cooking for us in the dorm kitchen. Mrs. Blackwell was off the hook, and I became a nurtured daughter. Gradually, my strength and confidence increased, making it easier to care for the baby.

Nine days later we were all ready to move on. Mom drove to wherever she'd been staying during her break from Dad, and Schmitty, our good friend from Union Colony, transported my son and me to the airport. It was my first flight in a commercial plane, and I was excited and nervous. I had prepared myself for the challenge of changing David's diapers in the seat and feeding and burping him in front of other people. He surprised me by sleeping through the whole trip.

DENNY MET US AT THE AIRPORT IN WICHITA, UNAWARE OF THE DESPAIR I'd experienced during the two days the baby and I were on our own. I planned to share it with him later, but I didn't want to spoil the happy feeling of being reunited. It felt so good to be together again that everything seemed dreamy and unreal.

He hugged me tight and then stared at his son's face and said, "Gosh, he's changed so much. He's fluffed up, and his head is rounder." I was glad he noticed. I'd worked diligently to coax that point down where it belonged, always worried about squashing his brain by rubbing too hard.

We got ourselves settled in the car, and I cradled the baby in my arms during the long drive to my in-laws' home in St. John, Kansas, where David and I would stay for a week.

That night, our son had another colic attack and couldn't stop crying. Den picked him up and paced back and forth, trying to sooth our screaming child, just as I had done in the dorm. With helplessness in his voice, he asked, "What shall I do?" His mom soon came to the rescue. She had raised five children, and this was no big deal to her. She warmed a towel in the oven and placed it under the baby's stomach. As he lay face down on her lap, she patted his back and then turned him over, draped the warmed towel over his tummy, and patted in a counterclockwise direction. It seemed old-timey, but it worked.

I was again in the company of a caregiver. I had read that a new mother was treated like a queen in some tribes in Africa, and the other mothers took care of her needs and those of the baby. That's how I felt, like an African queen.

On Monday, my husband returned to Emporia and his new job. My mother-in-law took me to her doctor because my stitches still hurt something awful. He put my legs in the stirrups, took a look, and said, "Oh, my goodness, you really have some birth injuries here."

I knew something had happened the day I fell in the bathroom, and his tone scared me. I asked, "What's wrong?"

"Well, you have a lot of stitches inside and out, and they're broken and infected. But don't you worry. We can fix this." He gave me a shot and sent me back to my in-laws' house with an assortment of pills and some medicine to put in the tub for sitz baths. For good measure, he gave me an inflated ring to sit on. The ring relieved the pain from my tender parts by keeping my tailbone elevated.

With all that nurturing, I started to heal. Then one morning I woke with two hard, hot mounds where my breasts used to be. They hurt so bad it frightened me. I asked Mother Auchard, "Are my breasts infected, too?"

"No, they're not infected. Pills or no pills, your milk has been delivered ... all at once."

I hadn't expected humor from my reserved mother-in-law. It made me laugh, and laughing made my breasts jiggle. They ached so bad that it set my teeth on edge. Holding the baby made them hurt, too, and so did bending over. It was a strange and unwelcome experience. She bound my chest with a dish towel and held it in place with many safety pins. It was so tight I couldn't take a deep breath.

When the temperature in St. John rose to 101 degrees, she gave me ice cubes to suck on. It kept me from drinking an excess of water, which she said was the cause of my swollen breasts. Having all that milk and good-for-nothing nipples broke my heart.

A week later, Den returned to take us to our apartment in Emporia. With a still-painful tailbone and healing stitches, I feared being on my own again. I wasn't ready.

Denny's mom read my mind and said, "I think Betty still needs assistance, so maybe I should go with you and help her out for one more week." I'd heard that a new mother needed all the pampering she could get, and that's what I was getting.

CHAPTER 28

Revealing Family Secrets

REFLECTING ON THESE EXPERIENCES MAKES ME WONDER HOW firstborn children survive the care of their parents. It's also a wonder first-time *parents* survive the experience. We had so much to learn about infant care that we tried too hard. Even then, we didn't know what we were doing. We made it up as we went along.

For example, we wanted our boy to have all the nourishment he could get and awakened him daily for a 3:00 a.m. bottle. It wore us out, but we thought we were doing the right thing. After two months of that kind of nonsense, Denny asked, "Would we be bad parents if we didn't set the alarm tonight?" We took turns feeling guilty, thinking our son wouldn't have enough sustenance, but I finally said, "Okay, we won't set it tonight, but I hope by morning he's not too weak to wake up." Without our interference, David slept until 5:00 a.m. From then on, we let him sleep until his body said, "It's time to cry."

David's head grew beautifully round, and the skin on his temples healed, as did his circumcision. Long, hard crying had caused his tummy button to stick out, so I pushed it back in and taped it down so it would stay where it belonged.

Our apartment did not have a washing machine, which meant I had to scrub diapers on a washboard in the bathtub like my mom did in the old days. I rinsed and wrung out each diaper by hand and hung them to dry on the outside clothesline. That primitive method left my knuckles swollen and red. Life got better real fast after we bought a Kenmore washing machine.

185

For six months, I slept with a board under the mattress, and I sat on my inflated pillow long after the stitches healed. My tailbone continued to bother me, and it took longer than six months to sit up straight instead of balancing on my left hip. The reason I'd had no painful contractions during David's birth remained a mystery.

THE PAIN OF CHILDBIRTH DOESN'T STOP MOST WOMEN FROM HAVING more children, and it didn't stop me either. We had always planned to have four. Five children in his family and three in mine meant that four would kind of balance things.

Soon after David turned eighteen months old, a daughter we named Rhoda came into the world. We nicknamed her Dodie. Her entrance was nothing like her brother's. With my first girl, I experienced normal labor and the joy of breastfeeding. When Dodie's tummy was full, she fell asleep, and I would return her to the "bassinette," a borrowed baby buggy. Her big brother often peeked over the edge to see what she was doing. One day he dropped his toy cars and trucks in around her. He meant to share them, but it appeared she'd been mowed down by miniature vehicles.

Dodie was three years old when her sister, Renee, arrived. Whenever I breastfed our new baby, big sister sat beside me on the couch and breastfed her doll. When I switched sides, she did the same, flipping her dolly into its new position and announcing, "Change sides."

When our youngest turned three and a half, we welcomed Bobby, our last child. By then, our baby girl had turned into my helper. She learned how to unload the bottom shelf of the dishwasher and how to stick safety pins into a bar of Ivory soap so they would glide easily through her baby brother's diaper.

OUR FOUR CHILDREN WERE SO DIFFERENT FROM EACH OTHER IN LOOKS and personalities that it seemed we'd adopted all of them. It sometimes reminded me of my role as a "surrogate" mother in the York

College dormitory. I'd moved into their world and discovered those guys were spirited jokesters. It drove me crazy. Then I grew up, had a family of my own, and discovered that my biological offspring were no different. In fact, they played tricks on people that made my college boys look tame. I feel weary just thinking about it now.

David once held his little brother captive in the closet and told him the man with creepy eyes was coming to get him. All six of us had watched an old movie starring Ray Milland titled *The Man with the X-Ray Eyes.* It had scared the wits out of Bobby. I scolded Dave for terrifying his little brother, so he targeted Dodie instead. He would hold her down, gather a lot of spit in his mouth, and then let out a long strand that almost touched her face. He usually sucked it back up before it made contact. When no one was looking, he did that to Bobby, too.

Dodie continued where David left off by resurrecting a prank I'd played on my sister when we were kids. Dodie waited until the lights were out to engage her younger sister in conversation. In the middle of a sentence in the pitch dark room, big sister would suddenly go silent. It drove Renee nuts. She'd say, "What? Why did you stop? What's wrong? Where are you? I'm gonna tell Mom!" By then, the perpetrator had to break down and giggle.

Renee played tricks on all of us. She loved to bake, so the house often smelled like cake. One day the fragrance enticed Dave into the kitchen. He said, "Smells good. When can we eat it?"

She could never keep quiet, so the temptation to share her little surprise with her oldest brother was more than she could resist. She said, "It won't be long now, but I'll let you in on a secret. I put a paper clip in the batter, and whoever gets it will win a prize."

Dave was horrified and said, "That's dangerous! Somebody could break a tooth or choke on it." She'd expected him to tell her it was a great idea, so his criticism shocked her.

After the cake cooled, he made her tear it apart to find the foreign object. He got the biggest chunks, and the rest of us ate what was left with our fingers. We wouldn't think of throwing away cake no matter how odd it looked. After that, Renee added less risky items such as an olive or chunk of celery to the batter, but she'd learned not to let her brother in on any surprises.

Bobby learned so much about tricks from his three siblings that he went beyond anything they'd ever dreamed up. When he was ten, he carried out his worst prank. It required a fresh dog dropping, courtesy of our German shepherd. Bobby and his best (human) friend placed a paper sack containing the poo by the front door of a cranky neighbor. They set the bag on fire, rang the doorbell, and hid behind the bushes. Out came Mr. Cranky, who immediately stomped the fire out with his feet. It didn't take long for the man to realize what he was stomping on. Fortunately for our youngest son, he was too old to spank by the time we heard about that trick. It's no wonder Bob was voted class clown in high school.

DENNY AND I LEARNED A LOT ABOUT FAMILY SECRETS ON OUR FORTI-eth wedding anniversary. Our four kids agreed to come clean while answering the question, "What have you done that Mom and Dad never knew about?" Adults by then, each one confessed to a list of sins, neatly solving several mysteries in the Auchard household.

When they first happen, mischievous activities provide little humor for the targets, but they make great tales to share when victims and perpetrators have all left home.

My family's confessions reminded me again of the twelve college boys who enjoyed being imps. None of the boys in the dorm had ever fessed up to anything, so whoever hid our bedroom key or stuck that embarrassing note on our bedroom ceiling is likely to remain a secret for all time.

But who were we to talk? No one at York College ever found out that we had hidden wine in our refrigerator. That is … until now. I'm sure word will get around.

The Auchard Family, 1961

Afterword

After our four children came along, it took a few years to realize that my first lessons in motherhood had come from the twelve young men in Thompson Hall. I don't know if they made me a better mother, but there were fewer surprises.

My real children were as different from each other as those guys had been. David was a sage and Dodie, a butterfly. Renee was a worrywart, and Bob was a clown. They were sometimes as ornery as the York boys, too. However, Renee, our "good" girl, seldom qualified for punishment. Dave occasionally needed discipline when he was young, but he wised up as a teenager. Dodie had a quiet way of challenging authority. If there had been a trophy for misbehaving, she would have won it, but her misdeeds didn't make headlines. They usually went unnoticed until long after the transgression, usually when the impulse to come clean inspired her. Bob was often in borderline trouble at school but rarely received punishment. Like Dodie, he knew how to elude the punishers.

Denny and I generally compromised on how to deal with the guilty parties when they did something that really upset us. He was the calm parent, keeping a level head and not showing his emotions. I was emotional. I lost my head a lot and showed my anger by crying. Eventually, I learned to tolerate a variety of behaviors from our offspring without drama. When Denny and I didn't agree on the way to handle an issue, we discussed our difference of opinion in hushed tones so we could present a united front for our darlings. We were giving ourselves and our kids private lessons in socially acceptable behavior.

When they were older, it was easier to reason with all of them. On weekends, each child had a chore assignment to finish before Monday. Sometimes they griped in a kidding way, saying, "Mom, what would you and Dad do without us slaves?" or "Shouldn't we be getting a raise for all this work?"

In 1959, we gave each child an allowance of a dime a week to spend or save. Renee once approached us for a raise. Her argument was summed up in two sentences. "Mom, a girl at school named Eunice gets a whole dollar every week for allowance. Why can't we?"

I said, "Honey, you're not Eunice." End of discussion.

When we did raise the allowance to a quarter, nine-year-old Dave saved his to spend during our vacation to the Badlands and the monuments of South Dakota. At the Devil's Tower gift shop, he found something for his dad that cost seventy-five cents, a decorative paddle with "Board of Education" printed across the front. Denny was a licensed psychologist and professor of education, and Dave felt grown up and "cool" for giving his dad a gift that mirrored his job. He assumed it would hang on the wall by his father's desk. Dave hadn't expected it to become a tool for punishment, but that's how his father used it. Two swats with the paddle was the end result of bad behavior, and each child eventually had a turn.

After our first child left home for college, Denny told friends that as soon as Dave was gone, I moved faster than a speeding bullet to turn the vacant bedroom into a sewing room. He vowed to be ready the next time a bedroom was vacated, but I always beat him to it. After all, he had two sheds and the garage for *his* stuff.

During the leaving-home phase, Dave, Dodie, and Renee took turns returning to home plate for a spell before getting back out there in the world. Bob, the youngest, stayed behind longer than the others for a good reason: he was single, still in school, and easier to live with than the first three. He was also available to help with manual labor.

Our kids lived within driving distance, so we stayed close even after they moved away. When we bought a motor home and traveled all over the United States for five months, Dave agreed to move into our house to avoid leaving it empty. No matter where we were, it was easy to find a phone booth so we could call home every week.

⚜

Dave

WHILE RAISING OUR FAMILY, THE SIX OF US GREW UP TOGETHER. Children change and so do parents, and we learned from each other. Now that I'm older, I look back on all our adventures and wonder how we got through them. Granted, it was a lot of work, but it left us with an abundance of cherished memories. I'll share a few of our favorites.

In the third grade, Dave announced at dinner that he hated liver.

Denny said, "Just take a few bites." Dave put a teeny bite in his mouth and then spit it out. Denny said, "It's not going to hurt you to chew and swallow it."

Dave put the morsel back in his mouth and then chewed, swallowed, and made a face. He followed that performance with a little speech. "My teacher, Mrs. Powell, said she didn't like spinach, but her dad made her eat it, and she threw up at the table."

Denny caved in and agreed that we would never insist that our son eat liver again. Dave didn't often win a dispute with his dad.

Den was the self-appointed barber for our sons, and he always gave them a buzz cut. Dave's hair had grown shaggy in the fifth grade, but he didn't want any of it cut off. He planned to comb it back on the sides and top and then pull his bangs forward to make a "waterfall" that stuck out over his forehead.

His father said, "No," and dropped the plastic poncho over Dave's shoulders. As he assembled the hair clippers with a #2 attachment, our son continued his protest. Though Dave gave up his argument as soon as the cutting began, tears ran down his face. It broke my heart, but Denny kept the clippers buzzing.

I knew how my husband felt, that a haircut labels a person. He did not want our son identifying himself with a trendy, goofy hairstyle.

Denny was strict but not heartless, and he made up for that huge disappointment by saying yes to Dave's next request. At eleven years of age, our firstborn developed a crush on the voluptuous thirteen-year-old girl next door. She belonged to the local swim club, so he was determined to join, too.

Denny said, "Why not? Let's see what the swim club is all about."

But our son didn't want his parents there. He preferred to ride with the neighbor girl's mom. If we wanted to see him swim, we'd have to sneak onto the pool deck, which we did. When it was Dave's turn to get onto the starting block, he looked cold, hunching his shoulders and holding his arms close to his body. Denny said, "Look how white he is compared to the other kids." He did, indeed, look pale; he also looked skinny. My husband felt the sun would do him some good, and I decided to fatten him up.

Because Dave was happier if we stayed home, we gave him some space. The day came when we couldn't stay away any longer and sneaked back to see how he was doing. The coach came over to introduce himself and asked who we were. When he learned we were Dave's parents, he sat down and said, "You folks ought to watch Dave compete sometime. He recently earned an A time."

Denny asked, "What's an A time?"

We soon learned all about competitive swimming, because our son had come to love swimming more than he loved the neighbor girl. He gave us permission to watch him at practice, and thus began our daily round trips to the pool. After weeks of swimming with the team, he looked different. He whipped up onto the starting block with the grace of an athlete and slipped smoothly into a diving position as though he'd been doing it all his life. Every visible bit of skin was golden, and his thighs had grown muscular. What an amazing transformation.

Dave's three siblings took turns following him into swim club membership, and Denny and I shared the job of getting the kids to practice and making them shower afterwards. Chlorinated pool water is hard on swimsuits, and we had to replace them often. So as not to be caught in a no-suit emergency, most swim team members owned two or three.

Treating our kids' ears with hydrogen peroxide to avoid infections became routine, and we got used to their bleached hair, which occasionally turned green. Being a swim parent was exhausting at times. On the positive side, our children were involved in an exciting and demanding sport and too tired to get into trouble … most of the time.

As teenagers, Dave and Dodie couldn't get along. We left the four kids alone one day, with Dave in charge, and gave Dodie strict orders to behave and not give her brother any trouble. Upon our return, Dave handed us a scathing two-page report about her rotten behavior. It ended with, "Dad and Mom, I was so upset that I had to play the 'Ave Maria' record to calm down."

Dodie was too old to spank but not too old to be grounded. Denny handled her grounding schedule, and I monitored her phone calls. A few years later, it dawned on me that Dodie and Dave had outgrown their conflicts.

After high school, Dave worked on his uncle's wheat farm in Kansas and then landed a job in a cabinet shop. He moved away for college and swam on a team that won NCAA Division 2 national championships in 1973 and 1974. After graduating from college, Dave taught high school and coached swimming; later, he worked in electronics. His current hobbies include wood turning and cycling. He and his wife raised two children, have six grandchildren, and are currently active in their local church and ministries.

Dodie

DODIE WAS FULL OF PISS AND VINEGAR, AS MY MOTHER USED TO SAY, and her naughty, wild behavior often earned her a warning: "When Dad gets home, you're gonna get it."

That's when Dave's "Board of Education" paddle would come off the wall, so I was surprised to hear Denny say we were giving it up. I asked why, and he said, "It takes a single swat for Dave to cry, and that's when I stop, but Dodie won't cry after two. I feel like I'm beating her up." That day the paddle became a permanent wall-hanging memento.

Proof of her determination never to cry happened the day the kitchen door closed on her finger, crushing the fingernail. Denny wrapped her hand in a towel and rushed her to the doctor while I stayed home with our toddler, Renee. When they returned, our injured girl was pale and quiet, with a bulky bandage covering her hand. I created a cozy place for her in the living room and then asked Denny for a report.

He said, "The doctor warned me to be prepared to hear Dodie crying, because he would have to remove her nail." I cringed. "They were in there for half an hour, but I never heard a peep. The Doc said, 'Mr. Auchard, I can't believe this. Your little girl made it through the procedure without making a sound.'"

I couldn't believe it myself and asked Dodie, "Honey, did it hurt?"

"Yes, it hurt bad," she said

"Did you cry?"

"No, I didn't cry."

"How could you keep from crying?"

"I'll show you." She demonstrated by lying on the floor on her back. "Each time it hurt bad, I raised my bottom up." She lifted her hips as high as she could and said, "Doing this helped me not to cry."

Dodie was a wiggle worm, and Denny told the future teachers in one of his classes about her tendency to keep moving. He said, "Your students will come from all kinds of families, so their behavior will be as different as you can possibly imagine. My own kids are no exception. My younger daughter walks across a room, while the other skips, hops, and dances. She never walks." It was true. Dodie started dancing every time she heard music, and holding her hand while walking required patience and stamina.

If motion was Dodie's first instinct, imagination was close behind. Her fascination with puppets made them her favorite Christmas and birthday gifts, and she created memorable stories for them to act out. Her dad hung an old sheet between the dining room and living room and cut a horizontal slit in the middle so a TV tray could serve as a stage.

After Dodie presented several puppet shows to our family, the rest of us wanted to get in on it. We recorded a script and music, and Denny built a wonderful three-sided portable theater. The little stage in the middle even had a curtain that opened and closed. We bought puppets and made puppets and hauled the folding stage to school and church to give programs. Our favorite show featured Madam Von Snootenberg singing in a musical titled *Tabasco and Tea*. Those shows are treasured memories, because the whole family took part.

Family was the center of Dodie's world, and she took her role as the big sister seriously. She and Renee were enjoying an afternoon at the roller rink when Dodie saw her little sister on the sidelines, crying her eyes out. She skated over and asked, "What's wrong?"

Renee said, "A boy was mean to me, so I yanked his collar and told him to leave me alone. I walked away, but he grabbed one of my pigtails and jerked my head back and punched me in the face three times.

Fuming, Dodie said, "Point him out."

As she glided toward the brat, she decided to scare the daylights out of him by talking tough and swearing. As a cussing novice, all she could come up with was "You ... *hell damn!*" I guess she told him.

Dodie continued to protect the helpless, even in her high school years. On the way home from classes one day, she passed a field where earth-moving equipment was in operation. She stopped when she heard yelling and realized that two boys were manhandling a smaller boy. She yelled, "Hey, you guys ... leave that kid alone!"

They were unimpressed and shouted back. "You can't tell us what to do!"

Enraged, Dodie ran toward the bullies. The smaller of the two tormenters escaped while the bigger bully dodged around mountains of dirt. Dodie finally caught him, pinned him down, and yelled, "Don't you *ever* pick on a little kid again!" When she said, "Ya hear me?" he nodded. She let him get up and told him to get outta there.

As soon as he was far enough away that she couldn't catch him again, he yelled, "Bitch!" and took off like a rocket. The boy's name-calling didn't discourage her. Instead, it made her more determined to help those who couldn't help themselves.

As a teenager, Dodie and her best friend created a summer neighborhood nursery school in our backyard. After high school, she landed a job at the Bear Valley ski resort, where she often cleaned the rooms where celebrities stayed. She later completed classes in child development and special education. She had a thirty-nine year career in Silicon Valley electronics, primarily as a Technical Trainer, developing training material. Dodie has three grown children and a granddaughter.

⁓⁜⁓

Renee

IN 1966, WE MOVED INTO A HOUSE WHERE RENEE, DAVE, DODIE, AND Bob would have their own bedrooms. Renee was nine, and leaving her friends behind in our old neighborhood was the saddest experience she'd ever faced. Her best friend, Nancy McGuckin, gave her a special going-away present, her own necklace, which Renee had always admired. It was a genuine plastic diamond in the shape of a heart. Renee couldn't believe Nancy would part with something she wore every day. Nancy explained. "I told my mother I wanted to buy a present for you, and she said I should give you something I love so it would have more meaning."

On the last day in the old neighborhood, Renee felt terribly sad and stood in our front yard saying goodbye to the air and trees. Nancy and another girl, Laurel Tracy, rode their bikes down the sidewalk, and Renee thought, *Oh no…she's already got a new best friend.* Her gloom deepened.

In the new house, Renee was so down in the dumps that she couldn't eat. Each evening she sat at the table with her head lowered, pushing food around with a fork until tears trickled down her cheeks. She was an emotional mess.

Denny and I couldn't figure out what to do, so he decided to talk to her privately. "Honey, what don't you like about our new house?"

"I like our house."

"Then why are you so sad all the time?"

"I miss my friends, and I don't know anyone here."

"Would it help get your mind off being sad if we decorated your room?"

Her face brightened. "Can I pick my own colors?"

"Sure, and a new bedspread …"

"And a pillow to match?"

It was good to see her smiling, but the other kids thought it wasn't fair for her to be first just because she whimpered and whined about missing her friends. Their dad convinced them it was better to see a happy face at the dinner table than watching her weep all the time.

When it seemed she was pulling out of her dinner-time blues, Renee had a minor setback. Denny asked, "Renee, why aren't you eating your pork chop?"

"I can't eat it."

"Why?"

"I have to save it."

"Why?"

"It's the exact same shape as the United States. I need to save it."

"You can't save it. You have to eat it."

Renee started to cry.

Her sister and brothers rolled their eyes.

Denny said, "If I take a picture of you and your pork chop, that'll be the same as saving it. Will you eat it then?"

With a heavy sigh, she agreed.

When Renee was twelve, we visited my dad in Iowa, and he let the kids help harvest food from his garden. They picked beans and several kinds of lettuce and then dug up carrots and potatoes. I was surprised to learn that our children didn't know carrots and potatoes grew underground. This new experience affected Renee more than her siblings. After she noticed that my father did not eat meat, she followed his example by becoming a vegetarian. She had no idea that my Dad's false teeth were in such bad shape that vegetables were the only thing he could chew.

Back in California, Denny helped Renee make our first garden, which prompted her to subscribe to *Organic Gardening* magazine. To trap snails, she poured beer into small bowls that she pushed into the dirt at ground level. She rolled newspapers into tubes and placed them around the garden. Earwigs climbed inside, and each morning she dumped them into sudsy water to kill them. She allowed no chemicals in her hallowed ground.

During her vegetarian period, she also found religion in a new church down the street. She started wearing overalls to school, with a bible in her backpack. The members at her new church prayed and sang in tongues. She confessed to me that she made up her own gibberish, suspecting that others might be doing the same. I shared all this with Den, and he said, "She'll be okay; don't worry about her."

Renee's tenderhearted regard for all living things extended to our newly adopted Great Dane, Simba. After the dog peed on our bed and ate our dinner straight out of the frying pan on the stove, we had decided to return her. Renee wrote a two-page, tear-soaked letter to Denny and me, begging us to keep Simba. Her letter was so heartfelt and sad that we couldn't ignore it. She vowed that she and Bob would share the care of that big dog, so we decided to keep it. Simba didn't leave until she went to doggie heaven at the age of twelve.

While attending college, Renee waitressed at local restaurants. She was then employed as a medical coder and Casefinder for the March of Dimes California Birth Defects Monitoring Program (CBDMP). Renee has two grown children and two grandchildren. She and her husband now live on a nine-acre organic farm with their chickens and goats. They sell eggs, goat milk, cheese, and produce.

Bob

When Bob, our youngest, was five months old, I noticed his little fingers plucking at something on the back of his head. I looked closer and saw how thin the hair was in that spot. He was soon diagnosed with Trichotillomania, a hair-picking disorder.

At two years of age, Bobby developed a new bald spot on top of his head. Denny was at a loss for a way to hide it, so he found a barber shop nearby where a nice guy knew how to hide the hairless spots under longer strands of hair. We continued to take Bobby there, because his good looks were more important than Denny's free buzz cuts.

Bob lisped and had an unusually hoarse voice for a little kid in the third grade. The school nurse assigned him to a speech therapist who saw her young clients every week. Denny was concerned about our son's hoarseness and asked his colleague, a speech therapy professor, to come to our house for a visit so he could hear Bobby talk. He said the hoarse voice was probably due to nodules on his vocal chords, which turned out to be the case. Our family doctor recommended that Bobby refrain from yelling or screaming. For some reason, that made him scream more than ever. The more he yelled, the more anxious I became, assuming he'd eventually have no voice at all. Fortunately, time passed, the nodules disappeared, and he outgrew the lisp.

Bob joined our family of swimmers earlier in life than his siblings. He was three when we signed up for the Turtle Tots class, where parents took turns being in the pool with their child. As soon as Bobby was tall enough to keep his head above water, he advanced to competing in races during the summer swim program. He hadn't yet learned to breathe while swimming, so they put him in the lane by the wall so he could swim a few strokes and grab the edge of the gutter to lift his head and take a breath.

He'd grabbed the wall many times before reaching the end, where he noticed that some kids received ribbons. He thought the white one looked better than the red or blue, and that's what he aspired to win. Bobby didn't know the ribbons were given for first, second, and third place in the race. He just wanted a white ribbon.

He graduated to the middle lanes and breathed by rolling onto his back to catch a breath. When he earned first place and received a blue ribbon, he was very disappointed.

As soon as Bob learned to swim and breathe at the same time, he joined the swim club with his three siblings. He wasn't quite six years old when he was first allowed to compete at a local meet. The six-and-under kids were the first on the schedule to swim butterfly, Bobby's best stroke.

We were so excited about his first meet that Denny left work early and tried not to get a speeding ticket on the way to the pool. While still in the parking lot, we heard loud cheering that wouldn't stop, so we ran to the pool deck. Someone yelled to us over the cheering, "You missed it. Bobby won!" It still hurts that we didn't see him win that day.

My husband planned our summer vacations around the swim meet schedule. The year Bobby and his buddy Kevin were ten, they swam neck to neck in most races, and both boys hoped to win the trophy for their age group.

At the end of vacation that year, we visited Denny's Aunt Nina in Oregon. Renee and Bob were horsing around outside while Nina showed Dodie and me her favorite recipes. We were busy copying them when Renee and Bobby walked in.

His eyes were wide open with shock, and Renee was supporting his crooked right arm as though it were a precious object. In a calm voice, she said, "I think Bobby broke something."

I'm embarrassed to admit my first thought was that he would miss swim practice for a while and Kevin would win the trophy. I had become a little league swim Mom. Denny didn't get worked up about winning and losing, but I sometimes cried when Bobby lost a race. I didn't know then that there would be plenty of swim meets in his future, including the high school team and an Amateur Athletic Union (AAU) team.

In college, Bob majored in industrial technology. A relative suggested that he might like working in the sheet metal industry. Bob looked into training under the four-year union apprenticeship program, and learning a trade while getting paid appealed to him. Better yet, there were more opportunities for advancement. However, he would have to take academic leave from college.

Denny's disappointment was profound, as seeing all of our children finish college was his personal goal. However, Bob had done his research. Once he shared the details with his dad, Denny saw the logic and agreed to the plan.

Bob became an accomplished sheetmetal craftsman, graduating from college by way of the union and winning $3,000 for his senior research project. He is also a part-time instructor for the Sheetmetal Apprenticeship Program. For nine years, Bob has been a swim official *and also swims in the master's program. As a hobby, he creates one-of-a-kind custom bells for officials all over the country. He is married, and his college-age daughter holds a state record for the 200-yard breast stroke.*

※

Denny

DENNY'S CREDOS INCLUDED FIX IT, RESEARCH BEFORE BUYING, SAVE for the future, and don't cuss. He was meticulous about everything. His side of the bedroom was always neat and tidy. Mine was not. He helped with housework, and I helped with yard work, which meant our home, inside and out, was always presentable.

I had a few traits he had to get used to, such as being too outgoing at faculty functions. He said he never had a chance to talk. I said, "You've gotta learn how to butt in."

I felt that he over-planned vacations. Den always created a rigid schedule for everything, such as our daily destinations and how long we'd stay at each place. Under no circumstances would he consider skipping any destination so we could linger at another. We had to stay on schedule.

For our 35th anniversary, we decided to celebrate with a weekend trip. I said, "For once in our life together, let's just toss a few things in an overnight bag and start driving."

"Well, where are we going?"

"Let's decide that on the way."

"We need to make reservations to sleep somewhere."

"No, we don't. Let's take a chance and assume we'll find something."

"Betty, I don't know about this."

I wouldn't give up, but he finally did. Luckily, close to dinner time, we spotted the perfect place, with condos to rent and a restaurant. It was the only time in our fifty years together that we did *not* make reservations ahead of time.

DENNY NEVER SWORE, AND HE KEPT HIS EMOTIONS TO HIMSELF. HE was a magician who conjured up lost things. He was terrible at telling jokes, but he was always nice to my mother and rescued our kids whenever they needed help.

He was orderly and saved for the future. Denny also followed through. On the way to a drive-in movie one night, the kids argued and didn't stop when their father asked them to. Without saying another word, he slowed down, turned the car around, and drove back home. The kids were stunned, and I was disappointed. I really wanted to see that movie.

DENNY'S CULINARY SPECIALTIES WERE SATURDAY BREAKFASTS WITH coffee, orange juice, pancakes, bacon, and eggs. Christmas grab-bag gifts were purchased by Denny and nobody else. He made all our house repairs, put gas in our car, and paid the bills. When he died in 1998, I had never learned to fill the car or pay the bills.

Now that Denny is gone, I rely on Renee to find things I've lost. She conjures them up with ease if she's here, saying, "Dad helps me find stuff." If something needs to be repaired, Dave has picked up his dad's habit of dropping whatever he was doing to fix it. All four children inherited their dad's ability to fix almost anything.

When Dodie and Bob start making us laugh with their stories, it reminds us of how bad Denny was at telling jokes. He was so bad at it that his amazingly wrong punch lines were what made us laugh.

These days, everyone helps clean up the kitchen after a family gathering, and they load the dishwasher in a slapdash manner. For Denny, loading the dishwasher was a science. He arranged things to make optimum use of space. Silverware was carefully arranged so no spoons were ever spooning. His dishwasher-arranging skill rubbed off on me. So when my family isn't looking, I rearrange everything to make optimum use of space just as he did. If they see what I've done and ask, "Mom, why did you do that?," I tell them that Dad made me do it. His mark is everywhere, and as long as we're in this house, Denny's presence is here with us. We talk about him so often that sometimes it seems he never left.

The Auchard Family, 1998

EPILOGUE

MY FIRST BOOK, *DANCING IN MY NIGHTGOWN*, WAS PUBLISHED WHEN I was seventy-five. I'd written the stories on napkins and other scraps of paper as therapy after my husband died. Then I wrote about my Depression-era childhood, which led to *The Home for the Friendless* being published after I turned eighty. I completed the manuscript for *Living with Twelve Men* at the age of eighty-five.

I wonder what I'll do next.

Perhaps, since we have a severe water shortage in California, I'll get rid of the grass and throw myself into designing a front yard with native plants. Better yet, I could go back to walking daily before my body takes on the shape of my computer chair. And I can't forget that I have a large family of four children, eight grandchildren, and nine great grandchildren. I would like to spend more time with them while I still can.

I will no doubt try to do all of the above, but the additional stories I've started have been calling to me. One takes place after I returned to college at thirty-eight, planning to become an art teacher. In my sculpture class, the teacher selected ten students to pose nude for a body mold. I had no plan to be one of those students, but I didn't get to vote. I titled that story "The Statue."

I've also begun a collection of stories about my experience as an old/new teacher late in life. While I was observing classrooms as part of my training, an inquisitive kid asked, "Are you somebody's mother just visiting class?" I didn't have the nerve to admit I was a forty-two-year-old student teacher and replied, "Yes, I am." It was not a lie. He didn't give up and interrogated me until I admitted I was a teacher in training. "Aren't you a little old to start teaching?" he asked. Maybe I was.

I graduated from college the same week my oldest child graduated from high school and went on to teach art in high school, middle school, and adult education programs for twelve years. I refer to the middle-school stint as my gin-and-tonic period, because menopause and middle school are not a good mix. It was a love/hate relationship, but I managed to keep that job for two years. Occasionally, I cross paths with one of my students from those classes. They recognize me, but I don't recognize them, because they are now adults. It makes my heart happy when they say, "Mrs. A, you were my favorite teacher." I hope they're telling the truth.

I've jotted down stories about my grandchildren when they were young, and they still make me laugh. I want to illustrate the tales and give them to each grandchild now that they're young adults.

I'm not sure what I'll choose to do next, but I'm sure of one thing: I'll never be bored.

—Betty Auchard

York College

YORK COLLEGE, LOCATED ON THE NEBRASKA PRAIRIE FIFTY MILES from Lincoln, held its first classes in 1890. The students met in rented rooms above a dry goods store on the town square. Citizens of York, Nebraska, and members of the local Evangelical United Brethren church (EUB) sponsored the initial courses. As enrollment grew, classes moved to an open area nicknamed East Hill, where the first building was constructed in 1892. In 1953, financial problems forced the college to close. The Church of Christ purchased the property in 1956 and revived the institution, which continues to thrive today as a private four-year accredited college. As of September 2015, the 125-year-old institution anticipates completion of a grand edifice, the Performing Arts Center.

The Administration Building (Old Main)

The Administration Building, the first structure on the York College grounds, was built in 1892 at a cost of $20,339. The three floors included a basement, a gymnasium, offices, classrooms, a chapel, a library, and rooms for two literary societies: the Zetas and the Pals. Even after other buildings were added, Old Main continued as the center of the campus. In January 1951, fire destroyed the building. *(Chapter 15: "Flames and Ashes")*

Hulitt Hall

Thirty-eight years after Old Main was completed, growing enrollment forced York College to build Hulitt Hall, a three-story structure that was meant to function as a music conservatory. Over time it served many purposes for the growing college. Choir practice took place in the basement, while music classes were held on the first floor. The second and third floors housed male students. *(Chapter 15: "Flames and Ashes")*

For information about York College:
1. York College Web site: www.york.edu
2. *York College*, by Tim McNeese, Bev McNeese, and Christi Lones, published by Arcadia Campus as part of the Campus History series.

Lessons from the INTRODUCTION

VE Day
VICTORY OVER EUROPE (VE) DAY MARKED THE END OF WWII IN Europe and the unconditional surrender of Nazi Germany and its armed forces. Celebrations popped up all over America, but none matched the rejoicing in New York's Times Square.

Lessons from CHAPTER 1: "Falling in Love"

Missouri Synod Lutheran Church
THE MISSOURI SYNOD DIFFERS FROM OTHER LUTHERAN CHURCHES IN its interpretation and understanding of the Bible. Many Lutherans believe the authors were inspired by God, and their interpretations were open for examination. The Missouri Synod Lutherans require strict adherence to Biblical doctrine, because they believe the Bible is without error in all that it says. They hold to the scriptures of the Old and New Testaments, and the words serve as their only rule of faith and practice. Though the description of faith from both synods may sound the same, their beliefs and practices vary. The Missouri Synod Lutheran doctrine is restrictive, where other Lutherans are more flexible.

Tanning with Baby Oil and Iodine
UNTIL THE ADVENT OF COMMERCIAL SELF-TANNING LOTIONS AND TAN-ning beds, teens made do with a bottle of iodine and a large bottle

of baby oil. The two were mixed together and then spread on every inch of exposed skin. The homemade tanning accelerator got the job done. As the oil attracted the sun's rays, the iodine stained the skin to give the appearance of a rich tan. At the time, sunbathers weren't aware of the damage sun can do, and even though the iodine stain tended to hide the evidence, sunburns were a frequent result of the practice.

Lessons from CHAPTER 2: "Becoming Mrs. Auchard"

Brown Palace Hotel

BUILT IN DOWNTOWN DENVER ON 17TH AND BROADWAY AT A COST OF 1.6 million dollars, the triangular hotel has never closed since its 1892 opening. The enterprise was named for its original owner, the wealthy Henry C. Brown, who built it out of spite for the elegant Windsor Hotel in Denver. His resentment arose the day Henry entered the Windsor in his cowboy attire and was asked to leave. The Brown Palace surpassed the Windsor in elegance, boasting twenty-six hand-carved stone medallions on the seventh floor, each depicting a native Rocky Mountain animal. The hotel also featured the first atrium lobby in the nation and included balconies for eight floors. The hotel originally grew its own vegetables, provided its own meat and cream, generated its own electricity, and installed an incinerator for garbage and an artesian well. Famous guests included presidents and members of the performing arts. The hotel's marble bar remains famous today, and the current price for a room with queen bed plus bath, Wi-Fi, and a city view is around $379 per night.

Evangelical United Brethren Church (EUB)

THE UNITED BRETHREN CHURCH AND THE EVANGELICAL CHURCH merged to form the EUB church in 1946. In 1968, the EUB and Methodist Churches joined to form the new United Methodist Church.

Thompson Hall

THOMPSON HALL BEGAN AS AN EARLY NINETEENTH-CENTURY HOME AT 929 Kiplinger and 9th Avenue, across the street from York College. The college purchased it as a dorm in the late 1940s. It was named for Anna J. Thompson, beloved college registrar and treasurer. The building first served as an annex dormitory for freshman girls, and Mamie Long from the Home Economics department was the dorm mother for fourteen girls. After WWII, the GI Bill encouraged young men to return to college, at a time when student housing was scarce. The need for a girls' dorm resulted in the construction of Middlebrook Hall, and Thompson Hall became the campus home for twelve young men. The hall later transformed into a housing office and general gathering place for faculty before becoming the Development Office. In the 1980s, the college tore down Thompson Hall, replacing it with Thomas Hall, a block-long brick structure that became the boys' dorm.

Lessons from CHAPTER 4: "Forbidden Fun"

Blue Parrot Inn

THE BLUE PARROT INN OPENED IN THE 1920S AT 1718 BROADWAY IN Denver, Colorado, and changed hands twice. Charlot Ellers was the last owner. After purchasing the restaurant in the 1930s, Ellers added a sound system, amassing around 6,000 records by the early 1950s. The building was demolished shortly after it closed in 1953.

Elitch Gardens

BUILT IN 1890 ON SIXTEEN ACRES IN THE WEST HIGHLAND NEIGH-borhood of Denver, Elitch Gardens was originally a zoo. A theater was added in 1896, and it was there that movies were first shown to Colorado residents. In 1916, rides and floral gardens became Elitch attractions, along with a dance pavilion called the Trocadero Ballroom. Old Troc featured famous bands of the time, especially in the summer. The zoo portion closed in 1930. Forty-five years later, the ballroom was torn down, and dance fans mourned the demise of their favorite dance hall.

Elitch Gardens closed its original location at 38th and Tennyson in 1994. The park relocated that year to downtown Denver along the Platte River and in the shadow of Mile-High Stadium. It remains a popular destination, having been enlarged several times with new rides, a water park and concert venues.

The Historic Elitch Theater at the old location closed in 1991 and fell into disrepair, but in 2002 a citizens group formed a nonprofit foundation to bring it back. The theater is in use again as a community theater hosting films and cultural programs. It is a feature in the new residential neighborhood that was built on the former park land. The distinctive domed carousel pavilion is still there, too, and boasts a dance floor; the antique carousel moved with the other rides. A small section of the garden remains as a park on the corner of Tennyson and 38th.

Eddie Howard

SINGER EDDIE HOWARD STARTED A BAND IN 1939, AND THE GROUP soon scored a #1 single for "To Each His Own." Howard signed with Mercury Records in 1949 and produced a second #1 tune for that label: "It's No Sin." His last hit was "The Teen-Ager's Waltz," which made it onto the Billboard Top 100 list in 1955. Howard died in 1963 at the age of 48.

USS Lagarto

THE LAGARTO WAS ONE OF TWENTY SUBMARINES BUILT IN 1944 AT THE Manitowac Shipbuilders in Manitowoc, Wisconsin. They practiced maneuvers in the Great Lakes before floating down the Mississippi to New Orleans and then to Panama. The fleet of submarines, including the Lagarto and its eighty-six-man crew, reached Pearl Harbor on Christmas Day.

In January, training ended, and the fleet traveled to the Marianas, Saipan, and the Bonin Islands. Between December and May of 1945, the Lagarto and its fellow ships engaged in multiple exchanges of fire with Japanese ships, and many crewmen were surprised they had come out alive.

While in enemy waters, the subs stayed in contact at all times. On May 3, 1945, the submarine Baya sent hourly contacts to the Lagarto and received no response. On August 10, 1945, families were given the news that the Lagarto was overdue from patrol and presumed lost. A year later, the families received an official notice that their loved ones were presumed dead.

After the war, the countries involved in the conflict exchanged records for the sake of history. One post revealed that the Japanese minelayer Hatsutaka had attacked a submerged sub in thirty fathoms of water. It's assumed the submarine was the Lagarto. In spite of that information, the location of the sunken ship remained a mystery for sixty years.

In May 2005, British deep-sea divers discovered the Lagarto in 230 feet of water in the Gulf of Siam, now known as the Gulf of Thailand. The sunken ship was sitting upright on the ocean floor, with a large gap on the port bow, which suggested a depth charge was responsible for her sinking. An empty torpedo tube meant Lagarto had fired off a torpedo before she went down. In June, Navy divers photographed the wreck for six days to confirm that it was, indeed, the Lagarto. A detailed video of the sunken submarine, titled *The*

Lost is Found, can be viewed on YouTube at https://www.youtube.com/watch?v=AuCxCGoahEU.

Lesson from CHAPTER 6: "Measuring Up"

Making Butter in an Electric Mixer

Early settlers used a hand-powered churn to turn cream into butter, but when electric mixers became a common fixture in kitchens, cooks discovered an easier way. With a stand mixer and heavy cream, it took only half an hour to whip up a fresh batch of butter, salted or unsalted, depending on your preference. At one point in the process, the cream turns yellow, and buttermilk forms in the bowl. Once the butter clumps into small clusters, it's placed in a colander to drain off the buttermilk and kneaded gently to press out any remaining liquid. The butter is rinsed under cold water, and salt may be sprinkled on the clump and worked in by hand before forming the butter into the desired shape. If refrigerated, the butter will stay fresh for up to a week.

Lesson from CHAPTER 11: "Surrogate Sister"

Little Sir Echo

John S. Fearis and Laura R. Smith wrote "Little Sir Echo" in 1917. Many singers and orchestras produced the song, including Bing Crosby, Doris Day with the Barney Rapp Orchestra, and Guy Lombardo and his orchestra. Although the height of its popularity occurred in 1939, the tune has been recorded many times since then, including a version by the Wiggles in 2014.

Lessons from CHAPTER 13: "The Terrible Trip"

Cancer Diagnosis and Treatment in the 1940s and 1950s

AS OFTEN HAPPENS TODAY, CANCER DIAGNOSIS IN THE FORTIES AND fifties was confirmed by surgically removing a small sample of the tumor and sending it to a lab. The primary treatments involved surgery and/or radiotherapy. In addition to high-dose X-ray therapy, radioactive radon seeds might be implanted in the affected tissue. Surgical removal of malignant tumors sometimes involved amputation of an affected body part. In 1947, the FDA approved the first chemotherapy agent, a chemical based on mustard gas from WWI, which added a new treatment option to the oncologist's arsenal against cancer.

Greeley, Colorado

LOCATED SIXTY-FOUR MILES NORTH OF DENVER, GREELEY SITS ON land that was originally purchased by newspaper reporter Nathan Meeker in 1869 to begin an experimental utopian community. He named it Union Colony. The area is bounded by the South Platte River and the Cache la Poudre River, which runs through north Greeley. Eventually, Nathan Meeker changed the name of his colony to "Greeley" in honor of his mentor, Horace Greeley, editor of the *New York Tribune*. Horace Greeley was responsible for the phrase "Go West, young man." Greeley is now home to the University or Northern Colorado.

Lesson from CHAPTER 17: "After the Fire"

Colorado State College of Education

A "NORMAL SCHOOL" TO TRAIN TEACHERS WAS BUILT IN GREELEY, Colorado, in 1889. Students (mostly women) could earn a normal school credential right after high school graduation by taking a few classes and then jumping directly into teaching. Only two women graduated from Greeley's first class, but enrollment grew. Twelve years later, in 1911, the school was named the Colorado State Teachers College. The name changed in 1935 to the Colorado State College of Education. In 1957, the college became the Colorado State College. Since 1970, the institution has been known as the University of Northern Colorado (UNC).

Lesson from CHAPTER 18: "Blessed with Good Luck"

Union Colony Apartments

ON OCTOBER 18, 1946, DR. GEORGE WILLARD FRAZIER OF THE Colorado State College of Education, now the University of Northern Colorado, announced the purchase from Joseph C. Ewing of the thirty-six-unit Lafayette Apartments and Annex at 17th Street and 10th Avenue. The building would house faculty members and married veteran students. Located not far from campus, it was a popular place to live. As soon as any tenants moved out, their spot was immediately occupied. The name Union Colony honored the early settlers of Greeley, who called themselves the Union Colony.

Lesson from CHAPTER 19: "Denny's Ready"

Monfort Feed Lots

WARREN MONFORT LAUNCHED A BEEF OPERATION IN GREELEY, Colorado, and pioneered the feedlot method of raising cattle, along with W.H. Farr. By feeding sugar beet byproducts to the cattle, he made beef available throughout the year. Until the formation of feedlots, beef could be purchased only in the fall following the roundups that brought cattle in from the grasslands. Warren's son Ken took over Monfort of Colorado after his older brother was declared MIA in World War II. By 1950, the feedlot had the capacity to feed 8,000 cattle, making it one of the largest in the US. The Monfort family left a legacy by building the College of Business on the west campus of the University of Northern Colorado. Another legacy, Monfort Plaza, was dedicated on October 30, 2000. In addition, the Monfort Elementary School was named after Kenneth's parents, Warren and Edith, who were long-time teachers in Greeley and Weld County.

Lesson from CHAPTER 20: "Making Change"

Dust Bowl

THE PHENOMENON KNOWN AS THE DUST BOWL OCCURRED IN THE 1930s following a severe drought that arrived in three passes between 1934 and 1940. The farming practices of the time left the soil bare and unanchored, and the prolonged drought turned it to dust. Subsequent dust storms created billows of dirt that traveled long distances and greatly reduced visibility. The effects covered approximately one million acres, primarily in Texas and Oklahoma, but also affecting parts of Kansas, Colorado, and New Mexico.

Lessons from CHAPTER 21: "Passing Time"

Frog Test for Pregnancy

FROM THE EARLY 1930S THROUGH THE 1950S, THOUSANDS OF AFRICAN clawed frogs were exported across the world to help confirm human pregnancies. In the sixties, immunological test kits replaced the frog test. By the early seventies, the first over-the-counter test kits were sold in pharmacies. The testing process was complicated but effective. In 1988, simple one-step kits became available.

Pizza in America

ITALIAN IMMIGRANTS BROUGHT PIZZA TO THE US IN THE LATE NINE-teenth century, and the first pizza restaurants appeared in areas with large populations of Italians, such as New York and Chicago. The popularity of pizza increased following WWII, after Allied troops occupying Italy discovered the local pizzerias.

Lesson from CHAPTER 22: "The Scientific Method"

BBT Method of Fertility Charting

THE BASAL BODY TEMPERATURE (BBT) IS THE LOWEST TEMPERATURE a body reaches at rest. Because BBT usually occurs during sleep, the accepted practice is to measure the temperature as soon as an individual wakes and before any physical activity occurs. The pattern created by lower temperatures prior to ovulation followed by higher temperatures at the time of ovulation can be charted to determine the likelihood of fertility. Researchers in the 1940s through the 1960s created a variety of methods for charting and analyzing body temperature. Due to the complexity of the math involved, the BBT method didn't reach widespread popularity until the 1960s, when Professor John Marshall and the World Health Organization introduced a simplified version.

Lessons from CHAPTER 23: "Waiting and Planning"

Childbirth in the 1950s

UNTIL THE LATE 1930S, GIVING BIRTH WAS ACCOMPANIED BY A HIGH mortality rate. After the introduction of more hygienic procedures during childbirth, the mortality levels dropped. However, by 1950, the pendulum had swung in the direction of making childbirth too restrictive, and prospective mothers were given so much medication for pain that they were often unaware of giving birth. Husbands were barred from the delivery room. The war against infection also led to excessive practices that included shaving the woman's pubic hair, giving her a pre-delivery enema, and keeping babies away from their mothers in sterile nurseries.

Childbirth without Fear

A British obstetrician named Grantly Dick-Read believed that much of the pain a woman experiences during labor is the result of fear about giving birth and the muscle tension such fear creates. He was the first physician to suggest that breathing and relaxation exercises might make the delivery process more comfortable for women. Dick-Read wrote *Natural Childbirth* in 1933 and followed it with *Childbirth without Fear* in 1942. The most recent version of the 1942 book was published in 2013. His work formed the foundation for several methods of natural childbirth, including Lamaze.

Emporia State University

In 1863, the residents of Emporia, Kansas, established a normal school to train high school graduates as teachers so their children could be educated. In 1923, the school became the Kansas State Teachers College. The name was changed in 1974 to Emporia State College. Since 1977, the school has been known as Emporia State University.

Laundry in the 1940s and 1950s

Bluing: White fabric tends to take on a yellowish or grayish hue with wear, so housewives in the forties and fifties rinsed items in a tub of water containing a small amount of bluing to counteract the dinginess. Well-known brands included Reckitt's Bag Blue and Mrs. Stewart's Liquid Bluing. Although the popularity of bluing declined as detergent quality improved, it remains in use today.

Starching: In an era when almost all garments and other fabric items in a household were ironed, starching was a common practice. Not only did starch make garments easier to iron, but it gave them the crisp body that was in fashion at the time. As a bonus, dirt didn't cling as easily to starched fabric. Before the advent of spray starch, it was necessary to dissolve cornstarch in hot water and add the mixture to the rinse water. After starched clothing dried, a housewife sprinkled it with water, rolled it into a compact shape, and let it sit for several hours (sometimes in the refrigerator) before ironing.

Lesson from CHAPTER 24: "Waiting and Creating"

Gordon Hall

GORDON HALL, CONSTRUCTED IN 1921, WAS ONE OF THREE RESIDENCE halls for women at the State Teachers College in Greeley, Colorado. Snyder Hall was added in 1936. In late 1950, the State Teachers College, by then known as Northern Colorado University (NCU), expanded into a nearby property once known as the Petrican Family Farm. The former resident halls on central campus are now designated as a state historical district.

Lesson from CHAPTER 25: "Hello, Baby"

Denny Dimwit

THE COMIC STRIP *WINNIE WINKLE* RAN FROM 1920 TO 1996. THE MAIN character was a woman who worked to support her family, including her parents and adopted brother, Perry. Perry came from a low-income neighborhood and continued to visit his old friends, the Rinkydinks. Denny Dimwit, portrayed as a dunce, was a member of the local gang. His pointed head and similarly shaped hat, along with large, floppy ears, made him a memorable character.

Lesson from CHAPTER 26: "Mom to the Rescue"

Pay Phones and Phone Booths
WILLIAM GRAY DESIGNED THE FIRST PHONE BOOTH IN 1889; THE UNIT included a system that allowed users to deposit coins after a call had been placed. The first booth was installed in a bank in Connecticut. In 1898, the first automatic "prepay" phone was installed in Chicago, and the prepay system became the norm for pay phones. It wasn't until 1905 that the first outdoor phone booth was put in place. By the 1950s, glass phone booths had replaced the original wooden structures. Also popularized in the 1950's was the three-slot pay-phone, which enabled callers to insert dimes, nickels, or quarters.

Lesson from CHAPTER 27: "Coming Clean"

Prices in 1950
IN 1950, A GALLON OF GAS COST EIGHTEEN CENTS, AND THE AVERAGE new car rang up for just over $1,500. A suitor would plunk down around $400 for a one-carat diamond ring, and his wool suit would have cost less than $30. Campbell's® tomato soup ran ten cents a can and coffee thirty-seven cents a pound. Sugar was forty-three cents for five pounds. A new house would set a family back $8,440. While those prices seem cheap by modern standards, the average yearly income in 1950 was less than $3,500.

Lesson from CHAPTER 28: "Revealing Family Secrets"

Ray Milland
MILLAND WAS A WELSH ACTOR WHO MOVED TO AMERICA, WHERE HIS movie career kept him busy from 1929 to 1985. Among his memorable films are *The Lost Weekend*, which earned him an Oscar for

his role as an alcoholic, and *Reap the Wild Wind*. Later came many more films and two thrillers, *Dial M for Murder* and the *Man with the X-ray Eyes*. In the latter film, which was popular in 1963, Milland starred as a doctor who experiments with eye drops that allow him to see through solid objects. He sees more than he thought possible, and the results of his creation led to disaster for the doctor who played with science.

Lessons from the AFTERWORD

Waterfall Haircut

IN THE 1950S AND 1960S, A HAIRCUT KNOWN AS THE "WATERFALL" was the rage. The style featured long hair toward the front that was allowed to fall over the forehead, often in a curl. It was popularized by celebrities like Elvis Presley and James Dean.

Betty Auchard

BETTY AUCHARD, A RETIRED ART TEACHER, WAS SIXTY-EIGHT WHEN widowhood prompted her to begin writing. At the age of seventy-five, she completed her first memoir, *Dancing in My Nightgown*, which became an IPPY Award (Independent Publisher) finalist. The *Home for the Friendless*, published when she was eighty, received first-place awards for content and book design from the National Independent Publisher Awards (NIEA). *Living with Twelve Men* is

224

Betty's 85th birthday present to herself, and she and her editor have already started work on a fourth book.

The oldest of three children, Betty grew up in the Midwest and spent the early years of married life in Nebraska. When her husband, Denny, landed a position as a college professor at San Jose State University, they relocated to the Bay Area of California, where they raised four children and a herd of grandchildren. Betty continues to write in the family home.